Scott Nilsson

Crafting A Bamboo Fly Rod

A Practical Guide to Making Your First Bamboo Fly Rod

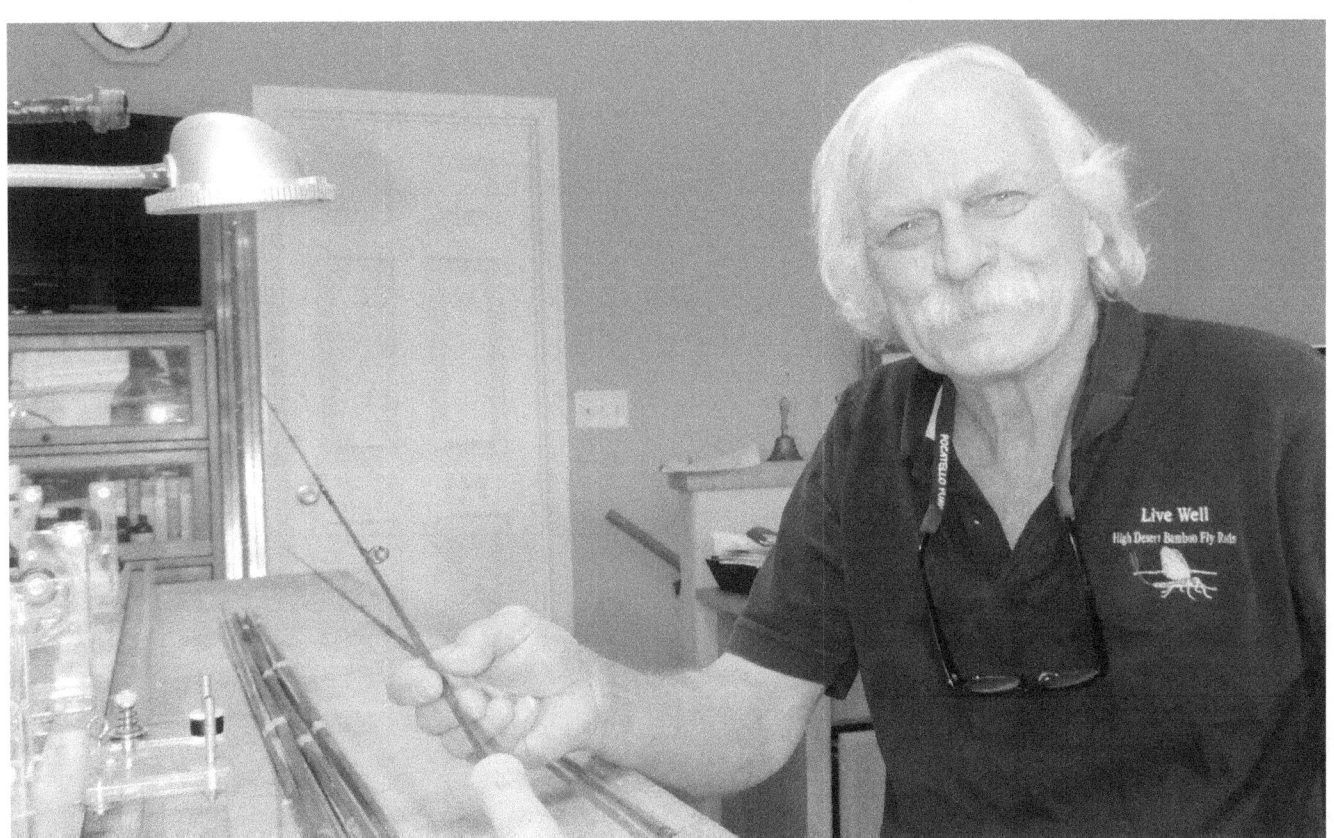

To George Harrington

When the only tool you have is a hammer, everything begins to look like a nail.

Lotfi Zadeh (1921) Mathematical Theorist

I graduated from the University of California in 1970 with a degree in Economics, hardly an education that would facilitate my career in making fine cane fly rods. I did, however, always love to tinker with mechanical things and found I was greatly rewarded when I could invest the time to figure out how to make something.

Resourcefulness, desire to succeed, and the ability to handle tools is an advantage, but only to this extent. Your fly rod will be either exquisite or will be simply just a great fishing tool. The more rods that you decide to make, the more your skill and familiarity with the process will improve. Your first experience and finished rod, will give you a sense of pride that you will never forget when you catch your first trout with the rod that you made yourself.

I think any person with a dream and persistence can accomplish great things and it is my firm belief that anyone that has some basic skills with tools can produce a fine bamboo fly rod. You may not even realize that you have those skills until you try. They could be buried somewhere in your make up and just waiting to be called upon. If you have dabbled in fly tying and were able to produce a fly that can catch fish, you would magnify that thrill exponentially if you were to make your own fly rod. You must, most importantly, have a strong desire to take on the project and to convince yourself that you can do it. You must be able to brush aside failures and believe in yourself. Bamboo fly rod building is not rocket science, although some would have you believe it is. It is my purpose to offer you some techniques and encouragement that will enable you to take on the challenge to make yourself a fine bamboo rod. You will have to be willing to invest in some important tools. You may have some of the necessary tools already in your shop. Some of the equipment required to make a rod can be made and some cannot. Who knows, if you continue to build rods you may be able to recover some of your cost

Acknowledgments

I would especially like to thank my friend, George Harrington, retired fish biologist, for motivating in taking on the endeavor of making bamboo fly rods. George and I were in my living room one evening with a bottle of *"Makers Mark"* by our side when he said, "Why don't you consider making bamboo fly rods." I was reluctant at first, however within a couple of weeks, I was on the computer researching what was required. I must also thank another friend, Gary Crist, who told me someday fly fishers would proudly say that they were fishing a "Nilsson". I owe Special thanks to Ed Suzuki, a former student, who offered help in editing this book. Many ideas, principles, results, methods and examples of applications presented in this book are either motivated by or borrowed from works cited in the Bibliography. The author wishes to express his gratitude to the authors of those works. In spite of my best efforts, some typographical errors will doubtlessly remain. Hope these are both few, and cause minimum confusion.

Contents

Preface

Acknowledgments

1	**Introduction**	9
2	**Buying and Selecting Bamboo**	11
	2.1 Buying and Selecting Bamboo	
	2.2 Choosing a Rod for Your First Project.	12-14
	2.2.1 One tip or two?	14
	2.2.2 Tapers? Weight?	14-21
	....	15-21
3	**Flaming Bamboo**	21-25
4	**Splitting the Bamboo**	25-29
5	**Spacing Your Nodes**	30-33
6	**Heating and Pressing the Nodes**	34-36
7	**Plane Selection**	37-39
8	**Sharpening Your Plane Iron with the Proper Tools**	40,42
9	**Rough Planing**	42,44
10	**Rough Planing Forms**	45-48
	10.1 Helpful Tricks	47-48
11	**Binders and Binding before Heat Treating**	50-55
	11.1 Getting Ready To Heat Treat	
	11.2 Using the Binder .... X-ing Pattern	
12	**Heat Treating Methods. A Simple Oven and Some Options**	56-62
	12.1 Constructing a Copper Pipe Oven	
	12.2 Note on Building the Butt Pipe	

12.3　Using the Copper Pipe Oven
12.4　An Electric Oven

13 The Metal Planing Form — **63-70**
13.1　Using Your Form before Planing Begins
13.2　Let's Start Planing

14 Planing tips — **71-75**
14.1　Final Planing

15 Planing Butt Strips — **76**

16 Preparing The Strips To Be Glued — **77,79**

17 Glue Selection. Mixing the Glue. Applying the Glue — **79,81**

18 Gluing — **81-90**
　Gluing the Butt Section
　　Gluing the Tip Section
　Removing String and Excess Glue

19 Relating the butt strips to the tip strips — **91-95**

20 Preparing the Ferrules — **96-105**
19.1　Marking the Blank before Fitting the Ferrule
19.2　Gluing the Ferrule
19.3　Bluing ferrules

21 Cork — **106 117**

20.1　Make or buy a cork press?
20.2　Forming the Cork on a Lathe

22 Straightening...Removing Bends from the Sections — **118 129**

23 Twists — **120**

24 Preparing Ferrules to Accept the Thread — **121,122**

25 Fitting the Ferrule — **123-126**
24.1　Preparing the Male Ferrule for a Proper Fit

26 Guide and Tip Top Locations	**127-130**
27 Wrapping Your Rod	**131-135**
28 Guide Preparation	**136-137**
29 Varnishing	**138-144**

    28.1 Wraps
    28.2 Setting Up a Varnish and Drying Area
    28.3 Other Methods to Finishing a Rod
    28.4 Dipping
    28.5 Second Dipping

30 Reel Seat Construction   **145-149**

31 Making a Mandrel   **150-156**
    30.1 Gluing On the Seat

32 Time to Be Proud Of Your Accomplishment   **157**

33 A Word on Fly Lines   **158**

34 Care of Your Bamboo Fly Rod   **159,160**

Appendices

A Suppliers   **161-163**

B Binder Plans   **164,165**

C Electric Heater Plans   **166-171**

Index   **172-176**

Bibliography   **177**

What People Say   **178,179**

Chapter 1

Introduction

This book was written primarily to encourage the non-professional craftsman. The purpose of this book is to help you on your journey to make a bamboo fly rod by minimizing frustration and confusion. It is intended to take some of the anxiety out of the process, which often prevents a fly fisher's desire to go ahead and make a fine bamboo rod. Making a fine bamboo fly rod is not as difficult as you may think. My son, Tor, made a fine rod when he was twelve years old.
When I started out making rods, I found an enormous amount of information out there, which can tend to overwhelm the novice. The books that I bought either wandered around from one topic to another, or they left some steps of building a bamboo fly rod unclear, or even unaddressed. You must read over each step and understand them before attempting them. There are simply too many things that must be performed correctly. If you decide to take on a rod building project I would suggest that you list the steps contained in this book. Write them out as this will help you learn the steps. Pin a sheet of paper above your workbench listing the steps and follow one at a time. I often get calls from novice builders who come over with problems because they did not follow this routine and forgot some of the important things that must be done before continuing on to the next step. You must read over each step and understand it before you attempt it. There are simply too many things that must be done correctly. You just can't wing it. Another thing to consider, which will pay dividends, is that if you find yourself getting frustrated or fatigued, set the project aside, go do something else and hit it again at a later time. You will be surprised how another day brings about more focus, and therefore, better results.
In my opinion, there is too often an over emphasis concerning the mystique and difficulty regarding the craft. Books on the subject are often cluttered with so much information that it results in fear and confusion to the otherwise capable novice. I am also a believer that one should take, with a grain of salt, the information to be found on the many bamboo fly rod forums. Forums can be helpful but they can also constipate your mind as well. Let me illustrate what I mean by sharing this example. I have a student who got confused about how to mix a material often used to glue the completed strips together, after he had spent a

considerable amount of time on one of these forums. He was convinced that he had to go out and buy special catalysts to add to the mix. He would also even have to use a digital scale to measure proportions for the mix before it would be suitable to use. This information only frustrated him, so he came to me for my opinion. After listening to his story, I asked him jokingly, if he was going to buy a white lab coat to wear before going on any further with the rod making process. I simply showed him my method of mixing the Urac 185 so that it had the consistency of molasses. I then glued up some strips while he was present. "I have never had a rod failure using this technique," I told him. We both had a good laugh over this experience.

This book will not contain many graphs, tables, or rigid building practices that must be adhered to. There will be no lengthy or extraneous discussion of history, comparisons of tools, methods or things such as what type of magnifying glasses to use. I want the reader to feel comfortable with being able to complete a good looking and fishable bamboo fly rod after he follows the principles set forth in the following pages. You can refer to the appendices where there will be references to detailed information in case you wish to go beyond a simple building process.

As trite as it may sound, focus on the KISS (keep it simple stupid) principle while working on your first project. Realize that you are not expected to possess the skill of some of the old master rod builders such as Everett Garrison, however you will have the advantage of using much more up to date and sophisticated tools than he used. Take the time to look at some of the plates in Garrison's book "A Master's Guide to Building a Bamboo Fly Rod"(. pp. 42 and 43) You will be amazed at the primitive nature of some of the tools that he used. Nevertheless, his rods are among the finest ever made. In my opinion, there are three reasons for this.

1. Garrison's attention to detail during the important steps.

2. The wonderful characteristics of the Tonkin Cane that he used.

3. His compulsive desire for experimentation, which established principles that we still use today.

After all, his book is considered to be the "Bible" of bamboo rod making. It is an accepted fact that these master builders developed tapers that set the standards for which the rods are made today. Their tapers can be tweaked with a bit, but these adjustments don't radically change the rod for the better.

Some of the steps in building a bamboo fly rod are critical and deserve much more attention than do others. There will be enough things to learn about. No need becoming overwhelmed with small details. I will do my best to point out to you how to make your experience as simple as it can be, while at the same time, minimizing your frustration. I have spent countless hours studying this process and have faced every imaginable pitfall. It is because of this experience, that I have been able to streamline and prioritize the steps required to make a bamboo rod.

The priorities that I consider to be critical would include the following, which will be discussed at length later on.

1. Selection of the rod that will suit your needs, including it's taper and choice of the materials used.

2. Selecting the proper bamboo culm to match the rod.

3. Establishing good sixty-degree angles during the rough planing process.

4. Proper heat treating to insure strength and prevent "sets"

5. Learning how to final plane to within one-thousandths of an inch or less by using the right plane and keeping the blade sharp. Also knowing when to use a scraper when you encounter a stubborn node or an uncooperative strip of bamboo.

It is a fact, and always will be, that as in any profession, there will be disagreements on the principles and techniques used to accomplish a goal. I am sure that in my profession, that there will be those who disagree with the methods that I use to construct a fine bamboo fly rod. It is their right to do so. My goal is to produce a fine, good looking fly rod that is fun to use, gives pleasure during its use, and is durable. I simply enjoy seeing a person make a bamboo fly rod when the techniques are translated to him in a manner that will assure his success. I have made many dozens of fly rods for customers throughout the United States. Those customers have given me comments that have made my adventure in making bamboo fly rods extremely rewarding.

Let's Get To Work

Before you decide to build a bamboo fly rod, you should consider this. You will be spending a lot more money to get set up with the tools required to make your own rod than you would spend on buying a rod from either me or some other capable fly rod maker. Unless you have a strong desire to make your own bamboo fly rod, and before you embark on this journey, you should give this fact some serious consideration. Another option would be to take a private class such as the one that I offer. This would be less expensive because you would be using my tools, however, with guidance, you would end up with a rod that you made yourself. If you are interested in taking a class, visit my website at highdesertbambooflyrods.com.

Chapter 2

Buying and Selecting Bamboo

So you want to build a bamboo fly rod. Where do you get Tonkin cane? A nursery? eBay? No, we are not after the kind of bamboo to be used as tree stakes.

2.1 Buying and Selecting Bamboo

The Tonkin Cane that you want has been grown and graded as far as quality is concerned, specifically to suit the fly rod builder. This accounts for only about 1% of the Tonkin that is shipped to the United States from China. There are two companies in the US that supply the fly rod builder. The Bamboo Broker in Seattle and Charles H. Demarest, Inc. located in

Cincinnati, Ohio.

The novice is not normally interested in large quantities sold in bundles (10 culms) or bales (20 culms). At the time of this writing the Demarest Company is the only supplier that can provide a minimum order of three pieces at an economical price. I do understand, however, that The Bamboo Broker now follows this practice. Prices range from $40 to $50 per culm. You might consider the larger diameter culms, which yield more strips in case you screw up some strips, and believe me, you will. These pieces can be shipped UPS if cut in half from the standard 12' length. Tonkin Cane acquired in bales and bundles are all 12' long and must be shipped by motor carrier. If you buy the more practically shipped and reasonably priced 6' sections, they will be well marked so you know which is the butt and tip sections. UPS charges depend on your location. You can check all of these prices by going to Charles H. Demarest or The Bamboo Broker website. Once at this site you can get much information about Tonkin Cane.

If you buy cane in 6' sections you will be building a two-piece fly rod. I do not recommend building a 3-piece rod for your first attempt, besides you would need a 12' length in order to do this.

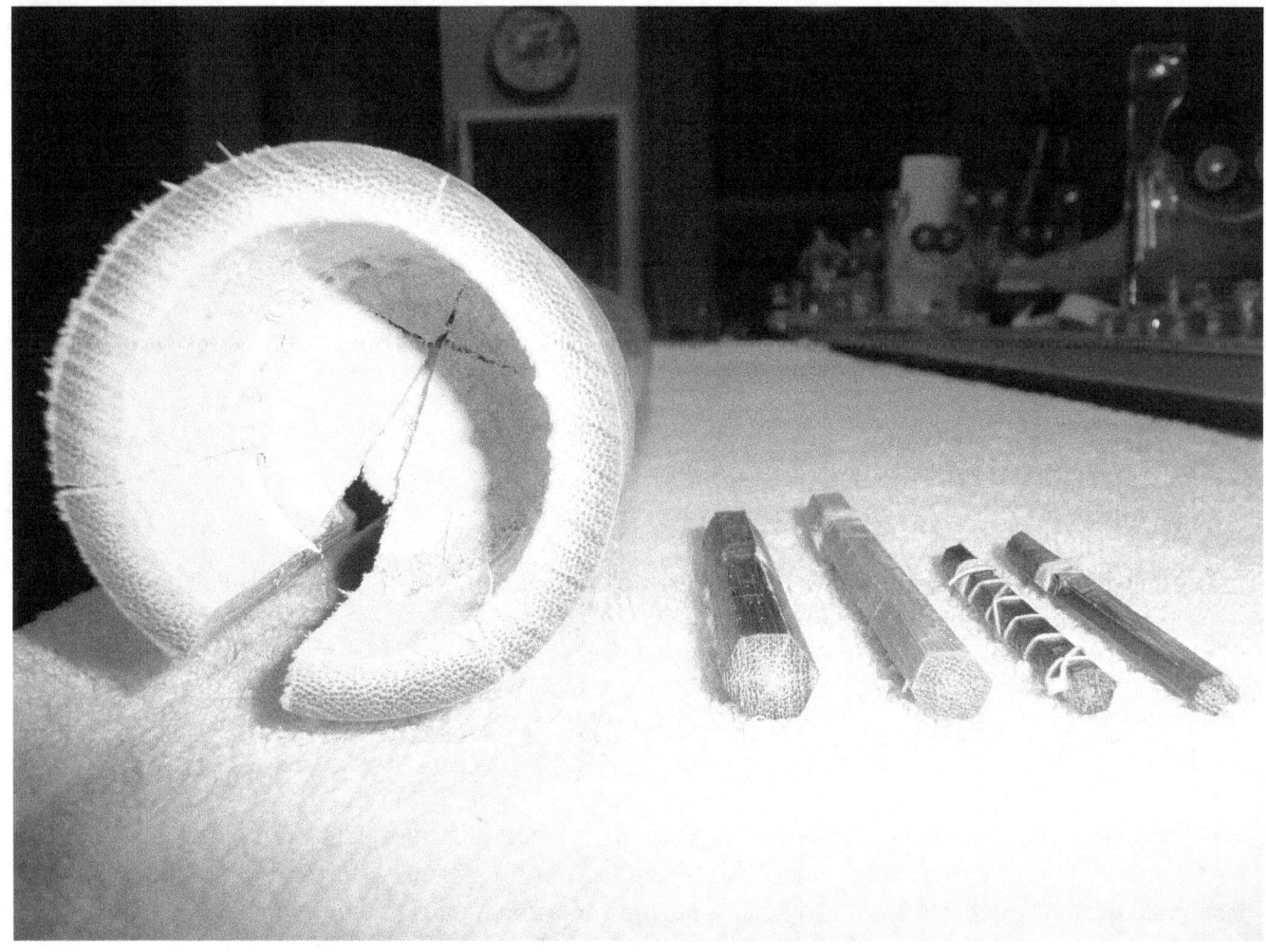

Figure 2.1: Culm and the hexagonal bamboo blank pieces

2.2 Choosing a Rod for Your First Project

Selection of a bamboo fly rod depends on several factors such as the type of fishing you intend to do. Considerations include the type of water you will be fishing, (small streams or large rivers). The size and species of fish that you after, what type of action you want in a rod.

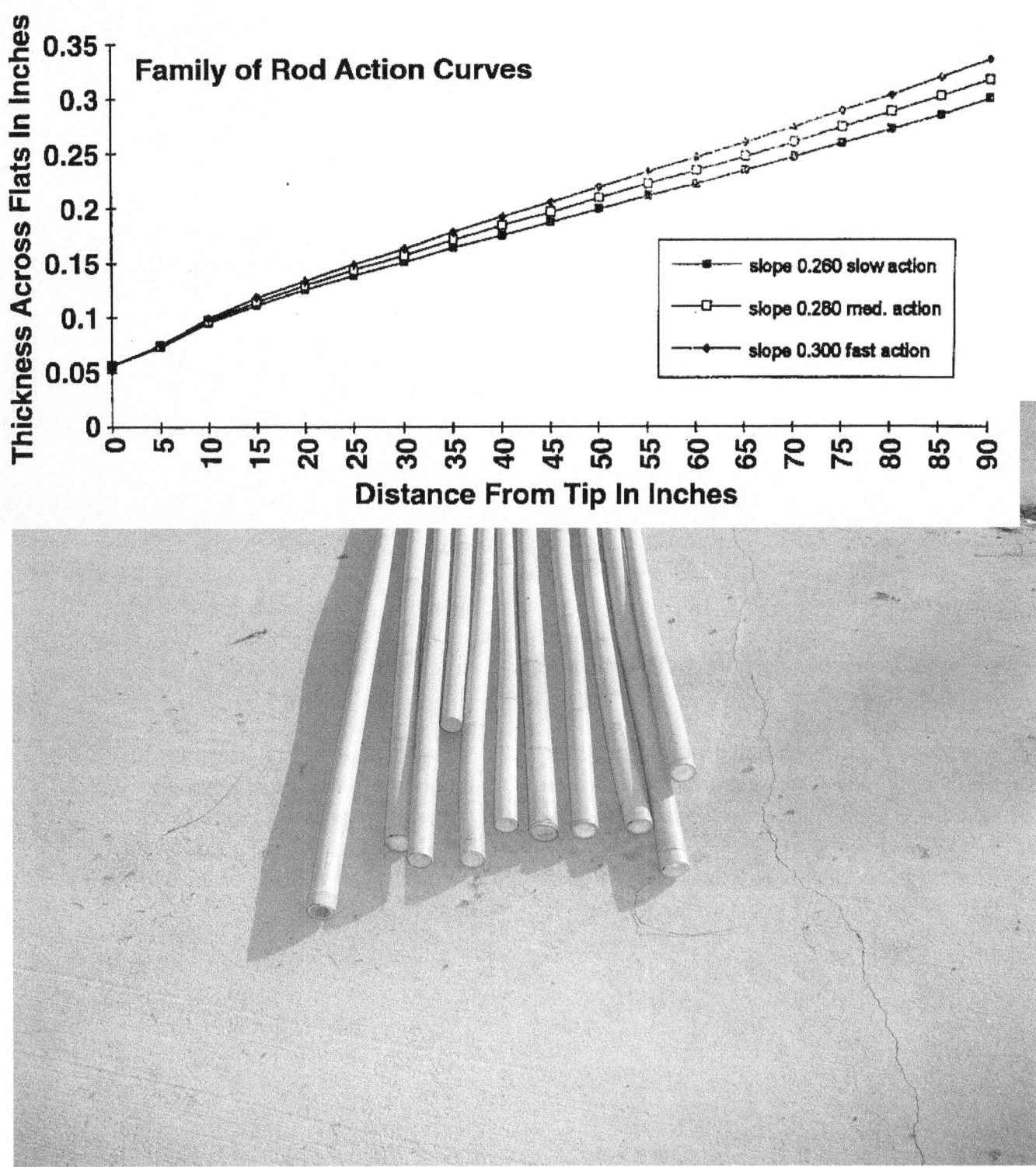

Fig.2.2: culms

It is impossible to have one rod that will meet all of your needs. Generally I have found that bamboo fly rods seem to excel in the smaller sizes. Since you will be building one rod for now, you will have to compromise. I do not recommend building a 6½' 3 wt. rod for your first attempt for the simple reason that you would be dealing with very small dimensions that would challenge the novice builder. For our purposes, I will offer three of my tapers. They will be an 8' 5 wt. a 7½' 5 wt. and a 7' 4wt. I recommend starting with one of the first two. If you decide to build a second, you would love the 7' rod, just a bit more difficult for the first attempt. You may contact me if you would like taper numbers for other rods

2.2.1 One tip or two?

Two tips are traditional, but not necessary with the modern glues available. Also, better heat treating techniques make the rods stronger and less likely to break. If you want to build a second tip I recommend that you label the culm you are using and set it aside.

The scope of this book will deal with traditional hex rods. When I was first investigating bamboo fly rods, I was skeptical about the ability of a short rod to be able to throw a long cast. I was a graphite fisherman back then and I was under the impression that fly rods had to be 9' long, or at least 8½'. I soon found out that bamboo throws a hell of a cast in the shorter lengths. Consequently, 3 piece 9' bamboo rods are simply too heavy to have fun with unless you want to get involved with hollow building or quads.

2.2.2   Tapers? Weight?

Tapers or the dimension measurements of the rod decrease as it goes from the handgrip to the tip, which determines the action of the fly rod. If you were to plot these dimensions on a graph for one particular rod design, you would put the length of the rod on the x-axis and the dimensions of the rod on the y-axis noting rod diameter decreases as it travels along the length of the rod. These measurements can be expressed as an angle. The greater or steeper the angle the faster action the rod will have. The rods that I build generally have medium fast-to-fast action. As you progress building rods you can experiment with your tapers and find ones that please you the most. If you are interested in plotting stress curves you can research them from a variety of sources found on the Internet.

Table 2.1: A favorite of mine

Taper for 8ft 5 wt. Bamboo Fly Rod SN: 8052

Tip section

Station #	Tip Form Depth inch	Total Tip Dia. inch
station 1	0.035	0.070
2	0.040	0.080
3	0.047	0.094
4	0.056	0.112
5	0.067	0.134
6	0.073	0.146
7	0.078	0.156
8	0.084	0.168
9	0.091	0.182
10	0.099	0.198

Butt section

Station #	Butt Form Setting inch	Total Butt Dia. inch
station 1		
2	0.113	0.226
3	0.118	0.236
4	0.124	0.248

station 1			
	5	0.129	0.258
	6	0.134	0.268
	7	0.140	0.28
	8	0.147	0.294
	9	0.189	0.378
	10	0.189	0.378

Tip-top guide size #5

Ferrule size 13/64th

Stripping guide 10mm

Butt Snake guides 2 x #2

Tip Snake guides 6 x #1

Guide spacing from tip to butt
Inches from tip of tip-top
4,1/4
9,1/4
18
27,1/8
34,5/8
40,5/8
52,1/4
64,1/8
71,0

Table 2.2: A fine trout rod

Taper for 7ft 6 inches 5 wt. Bamboo Fly Rod

Tip section

Station #	Tip Form Depth inch	Total Tip Dia. inch
station 1	0.035	0.70
2	0.040	0.80
3	0.046	0.92
4	0.057	114
5	0.067	0.134
6	0.073	0.146
7	0.078	0.155
8	0.085	0.170
9	0.091	0.182
10	0.102	0.204

Butt Section

Station #	Butt Form Depth inch	Total Butt Dia. inch

station 1		0.107	0.214
	2	0.113	0.226
	3	0.119	0.238
	4	0.123	0.246
	5	0.129	0.258
	6	0.136	0.272
	7	0.139	0.278
	8	0.180	0.360
	9	0.180	0.360
	10	0.180	0.360

Tip-top guide size = 4.5

Ferrule size 13/64th

Stripping guide 10mm

Butt Snake guides 2 x #2

Tip Snake guides 6 x #1

Guide spacing from tip to butt
Inches from tip of tip-top
4,3/4
10,5/8
16,5/8

22,5/8
33,3/8
41,1/2
49,3/4
57,1/2
65,3/8

Table 2.3: Great rod for small water

Taper for 7 ft. 4 wt. Bamboo Fly Rod SN: 7042

Tip section

Station #	Tip Form Depth inch	Total Tip Dia. inch
station 1	0.034	0.068
2	0.036	0.072

	3	0.042	0.084
	4	0.051	0.102
	5	0.062	0.124
	6	0.069	0.138
	7	0.076	0.152
	8	0.083	0.166
	9	0.092	0.184
	10		

Tip-top guide size = # 4.5

Ferrule size 12/64th

Stripping guide 10mm

Butt Snake guides 2 x #2

Tip Snake guides 6 x #1

Guide spacing from tip to butt
Inches from tip of tip-top
4,3/8
8,7/8
15
21,1/2
28,5/8
36,1/2
45,1/4
53
61,1/4

Butt Section

Station #	Butt Form Depth inch	Total Butt Dia. inch
station 1	0.104	0.208
2	0.107	0.214
3	0.110	0.222
4	0.123	0.246
5	0.126	0.252

6	0.129	0.258
8	0.136	0.272

Tip-top guide size = # 4.5

Ferrule size 12/64th

Stripping guide 10mm

Butt Snake guides 2 x #2

Tip Snake guides 6 x #1

Guide spacing from tip to butt

Inches from tip of tip-top
4,3/8
8,7/8
15
21,1/2
28,5/8
36,1/2
45,1/4
53
61,1/4

Chapter 3

Flaming Bamboo

Figure 3.1: Below-Torch with fine tip, weed burner attachment for 5 Gallon propane canister and BernzOmatic TS4000

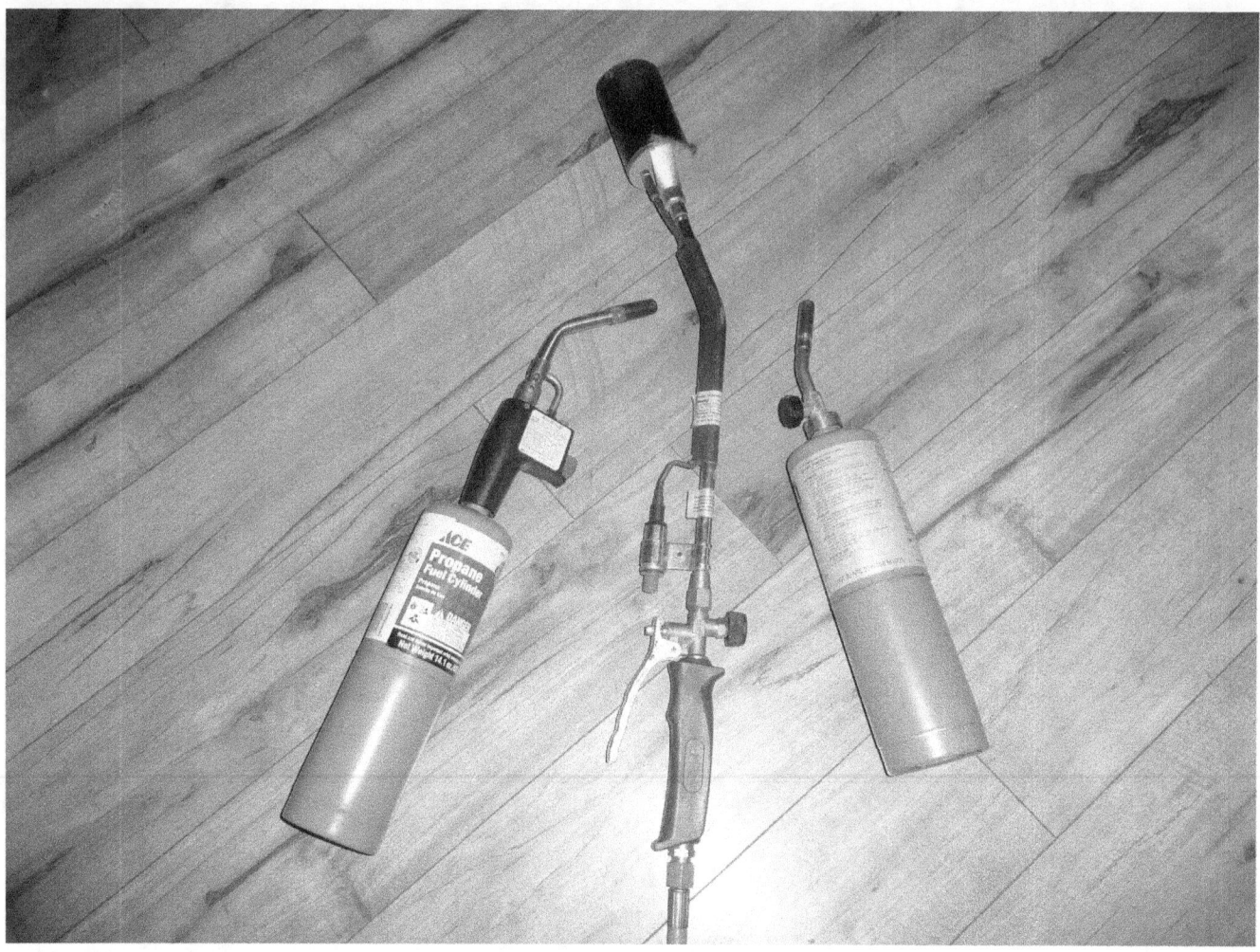

When I started making rods, I made blonde rods exclusively. They looked fine to me and required fewer steps to build them. I still make quite a few blonde rods, but as time went by I got more requests from customers for flamed or striped rods, often called tigers. I was also interested in experimenting. At one point I decided that blonde rods looked a bit anemic compared to a flamed or striped rod, but this is a matter of personal choice. I might add that you can eliminate the anemic look on blonde rods by heat-treating a bit longer, which will give the bamboo a richer tone. You can also use a chemical called potassium permanganate. It comes in a crystal form and is mixed with water. Each coat that is wiped on slowly darkens the cane. It is often used in fly rod restoration in order to match a replacement section of a broken flamed bamboo fly rod. If you do decide to color the rod, it is done before the culm is split. A weed burning propane torch is used. For striping, I use a BernzOmatic TS4000 for wide stripes and, I bought a pencil attachment for the same torch, which yields narrower stripes. These torches use the 14.1oz replacement propane canisters readily available at hardware stores.

Should you decide to flame your rod, I recommend a weed burning torch hooked up to a large propane canister such as those used on BBQs. Don't hesitate to put a charcoal like burn on the culm. The torch should produce a high enough temperature to char the outside, but not cook the inside, which could damage the power fibers. The burned culm will concern you but the color will be fine once the enamel is removed. Under doing the flaming may result in a lighter color than is desired once the enamel is removed. To accomplish the flaming I set my culm on two metal sawhorses and rotate the culm Using a channel lock pliers. Use an even stroke similar to spray painting, to get the color uniform. The darkness will be removed later when the enamel is removed using a razor blade. Remember, that if you under flame the outer surface your result will end up lighter than you might like. I recommend some practice on this. In order to check the color of your finished rod, Use a razor blade to scrap off some of the enamel.

Figure 3.2: Below-A flamed culm on p. 24

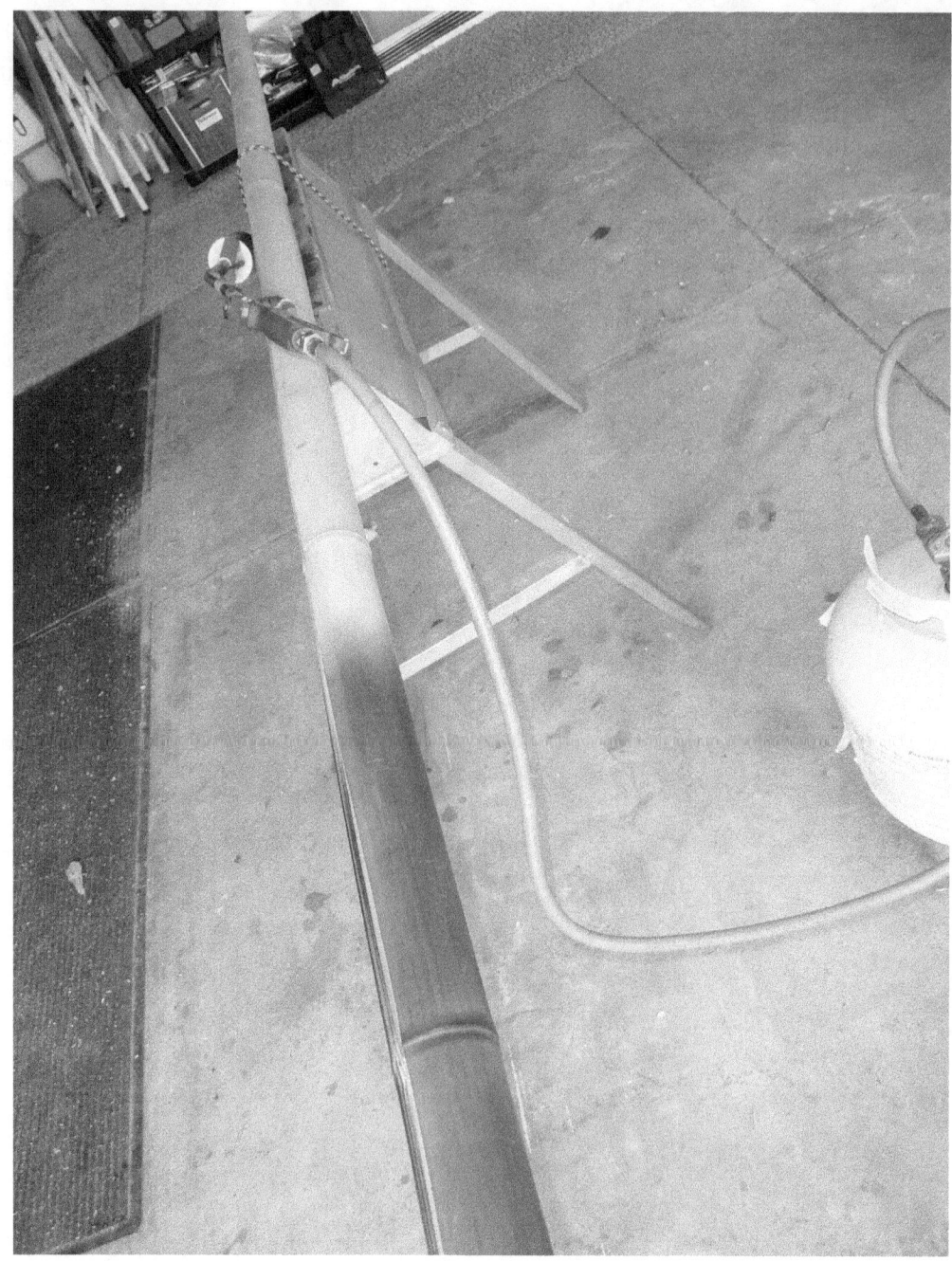

Use a razor blade to scrap off some of the enamel.

To accomplish the flaming, I set my culm on two metal sawhorses and rotate the culm using a channel lock pliers. Use an even stroke similar to spray painting, which makes for a uniform color. The charred look will be removed later when the enamel is removed using a razor blade. Remember, under flaming the outer surface will result in a lighter colored rod than you would like when the enamel is removed.

Faming should not be used as a substitute for heat-treating.

There is some debate out there, but I have found that flamed rods produce a bit more stiffness in the cast.

In fig 3.1 Torches from left to right.

1. Small tip for pencil sized lines.
2. Hi temp weed burner for flaming.
3. Pushbutton start TS 4000 for wide stripes. Moreover, it can be used for heat-treating using the pipe method discussed later in the heat treatment segment.

If you have some areas on the strips that appear too light, you can carefully touch up those spots on the strips using the fine nozzle torch. Be careful! Don't scorch the sides of the strips.

Chapter 4

Splitting the Bamboo

The power fibers that run the length of the bamboo culm are responsible for the finished rod's strength and wonderful casting characteristics. They could be compared to the many wires in the cables used on some suspension bridges, although they are not twisted together.
Refer to the cross section below or your bamboo culm, sanded at the butt end. You will notice that the power fibers become denser as they move away from the center of the culm. The more power fibers in a culm, the heavier the culm is. As you move towards the center of the culm you will notice that the power fibers become encircled with the light colored pith material. We want to make sure that the culm that we select for a particular rod size has enough dense power fibers to support that rod. The dimension of this dense area of power fiber area required, then, would be $\frac{1}{}$ the rod diameter, or the dimension of one finished strip. If the culm cannot meet this requirement it should be used for a smaller rod. Lack of enough power fibers will result in a weak fly rod. .

Identify the base of the culm where it grew out of the ground. This will become your

butt section and the top 6' of your culm will become your tip section. If you are working with two 6' pieces they will be clearly identified where they were cut by two similar numbers or letters that the supplier marked on them. This was the mid point of the culm. You will find as you go from base to the tip, the nodes become further apart. Also the base or bottom of the culm will have a much thicker wall than the tip or top of the culm. This will become your butt section and the top 6'of your culm will become your tip section. It is important to mark the base and mid point of the culm once it is cut in half . I use a black sharpie pen for the base and a red sharpie pen for the bottom of the tip (mid point of culm). This will also help you identify the strips later in the process. Usually the culms will have pre existing splits in them, they occur as the culm dries out. If this is the case and there is one split present, begin a new split 180° opposite of the existing split. You can purchase a froe to accomplish this, but a rubber mallet (Wooden one is fine also). an old Chinese meat cleaver will work just as well.

Start with splitting the 6' butt portion of the culm. Begin at the end that you have marked black, placing the other end against the bottom of a wall or step to keep it from sliding. Work the cleaver down the culm using the mallet to create a split. If the culm did not have an existing split you can create your first split using the process above. You will find that some culms have multiple splits or splits that don't go down the full length of the culm. In this case evaluate the culm and decide how best to get it into two halves. Once you have split the culm in half use the same process to split the two halves again that will yield four pieces. I do this a little differently from some rod makers who divide the two halves into 3 pieces before splitting those strips into more strips. I do this because I have decided to use a band saw to do the rest of the strip preparation. This is controversial in some circles, but what isn't in the process of building a bamboo rod. I have adapted methods that streamline the process and in no way do they produce an inferior rod. Do you interfere with the power fibers using the band saw? Hogwash is my answer. I have found that you get more uniform strips with less waste using my method. Often times with hand splitting, the blade wanders and just creates frustration. Try hand splitting if you want, but you will soon find out why I use the band saw. I use a ¼" blade with about 10 teeth per inch on my saw. Too few teeth make for too aggressive of a cut. BI metal is a good choice.

Using the band saw is a convenient way to remove the diaphragm material, shown in Fig. 4.7. After removing the diaphragm material, the piece won't hang up on the saw platform. Simply pass one of the four strips slowly through the blade making sure you are not drifting the blade from one side to the other. I do not use a fencing device when I cut strips. I make my butt strips about ½" wide and my tip strips about ¼" or slightly under. You might go slightly wider on your first rod. Just remember the wider they are the more you will have to hog off with the plane later. Don't worry about how many strips you can get out of one culm. I have seen this discussion at length on forums and it drives me nuts. Remember the approximate cost of materials in your rod will be about $150 and bamboo is about the least expensive of the materials. It's the nickel silver hardware that will eat you up, not the bamboo. One culm will

Culm Cross Section

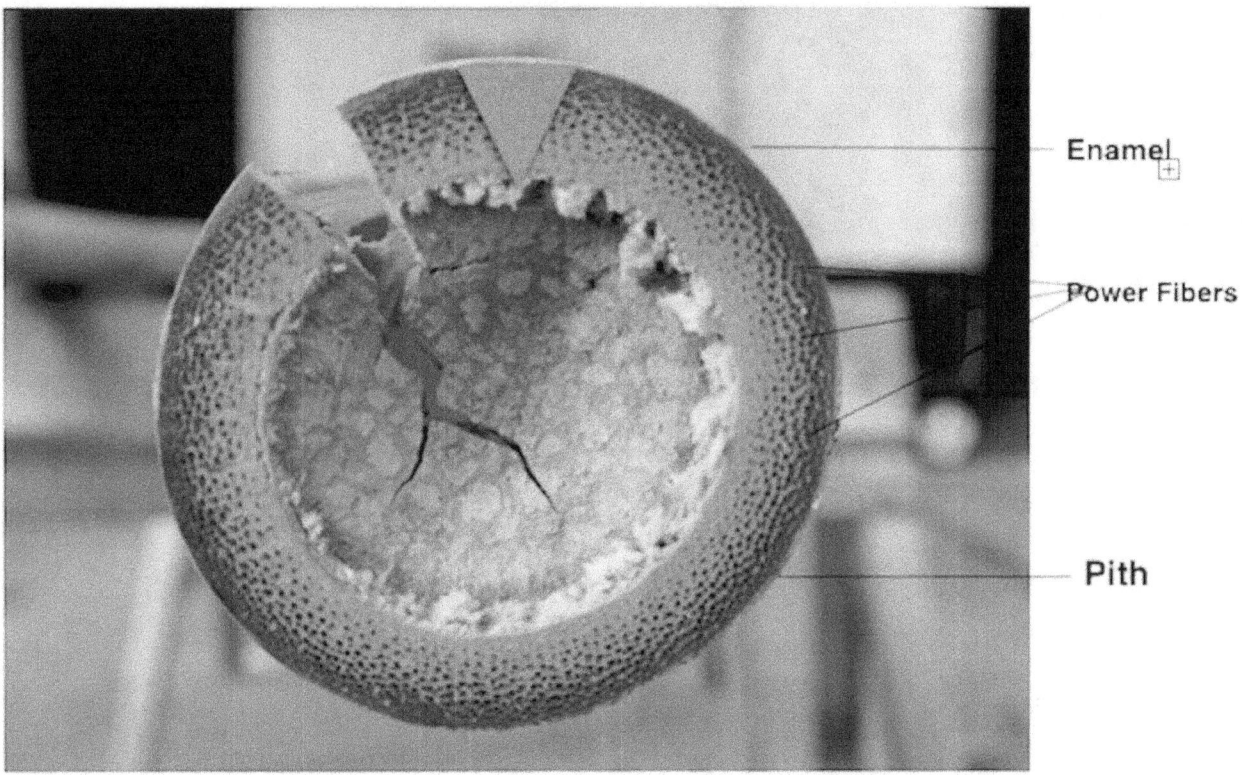

One culm will produce one two-tip rod. As you continue to cut strips you will have to remove more diaphragm material before you make narrower strips. Be sure to make two extra strips for the butt and tip and set them aside well labeled to easily identify them later. There is a high probability when making your first rod that you will need them later if you break a strip.

If you make a two-tip rod, make enough strips to accommodate the second tip. Two additional strips for each section are advised. When you have finished your strips check each one to make sure there are no imperfections on the enamel side of the strips. Sometimes culms will have divots or other irregularities that were caused from branches or parasites.

Note the divot area on the bottom of the culm on the left in fig. 4.6. These kinds of areas must be worked around by the rod maker and can't be present in a strip

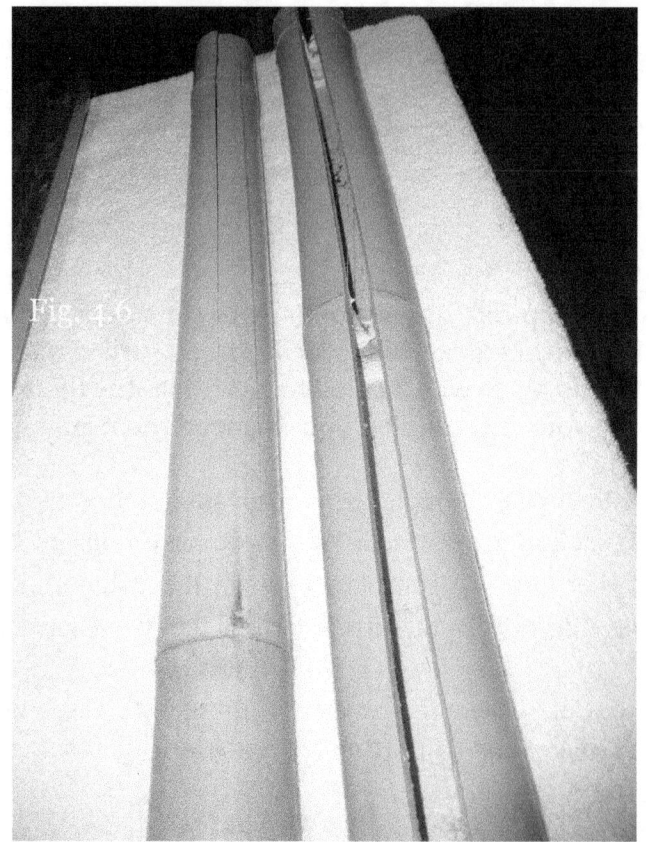

Fig. 4.6

Fig 4.7 Removing diaphragm material with the band saw

Chapter 5

Spacing Your Nodes

There are numerous techniques in which you can space nodes and many more arguments out there to justify one method over another. I would not be concerned about trying to make some sort of firing order arrangement as you find in a six-cylinder car engine. You will use more bamboo and become too confused about having to number each strip and worry about keeping those strips in order. I suggest the 3 × 3 method of node spacing made popular by the Leonard Rod Company. It is simple, strong and makes good use of the bamboo. I still use it today because no one has demonstrated other methods are superior.

I begin with the butt strips. Make sure that the diaphragm located on the pith side of the strip (opposite the enamel) has been sanded or filed relatively smooth. Take two strips and lay them down next to each other enamel side up. Move that second strip so that it is either up or down stream from the first strip so that there is about a 5" difference between the nodes on both strips. Now, just simply lay down the next strips to match the first two. You will then end up with two sets of strips, three in each set, having the same node locations. Fig. 5.1. 5.2. Make sure that the marked ends of the strips, whether tips or butts are all at the same end.

Next we will determine where you will cut the strips. The strips should be 3" longer on each end than ½ the finished rod section length. For example, if you are making a 7½' rod it will be 90" long in total. Since it is a two-piece rod, each section will be 45" long. Make the strips 51" long. You will see later why you will want to cut your strips about 6" longer. Fig. 5.3. Do this in a manner that will minimize the number of nodes on your strips.

Now it is time to repeat the process with the tip strips. If you make a two tip rod, make certain to space nodes on the additional six strips so that the two tips will have matching node spacing. Do not space nodes, or cut your extra strips. If you break a strip later you will have to match that broken strip's node spacing on one of the extra strips.

Now repeat the process above for the tip section. The only difference comes when you make the cut measurements. One of the characteristics of a well-made bamboo fly rod is that it should not have nodes close to the tip top. Fortunately the distance between nodes becomes greater as you move from the base of the culm up towards the tip area. Once you have the tip strips lying flat on your bench make sure that the cut mark that you will be placing at the tip end (down stream from red marked ferrule ends) is placed as far away as possible from a node. A node could be 2" below your cut mark because it will be cut off later since the strips are 3 inches longer at each end.

When both butt strips and tip strips have been marked for cutting, cut them either with the band saw or a fine blade saw such as a Japanese fine crosscut saw. Remember to re-mark the butt strips black towards the grip end and the tip strips red at the ferrule end since you will be cutting off the original marks present.

Figure 5.1: Node spacing

No nodes should be next to each other on adjacent strips. Note: Nodes on strips 1, 3, 5 should be 5 inches apart from strips 2, 4, 6.

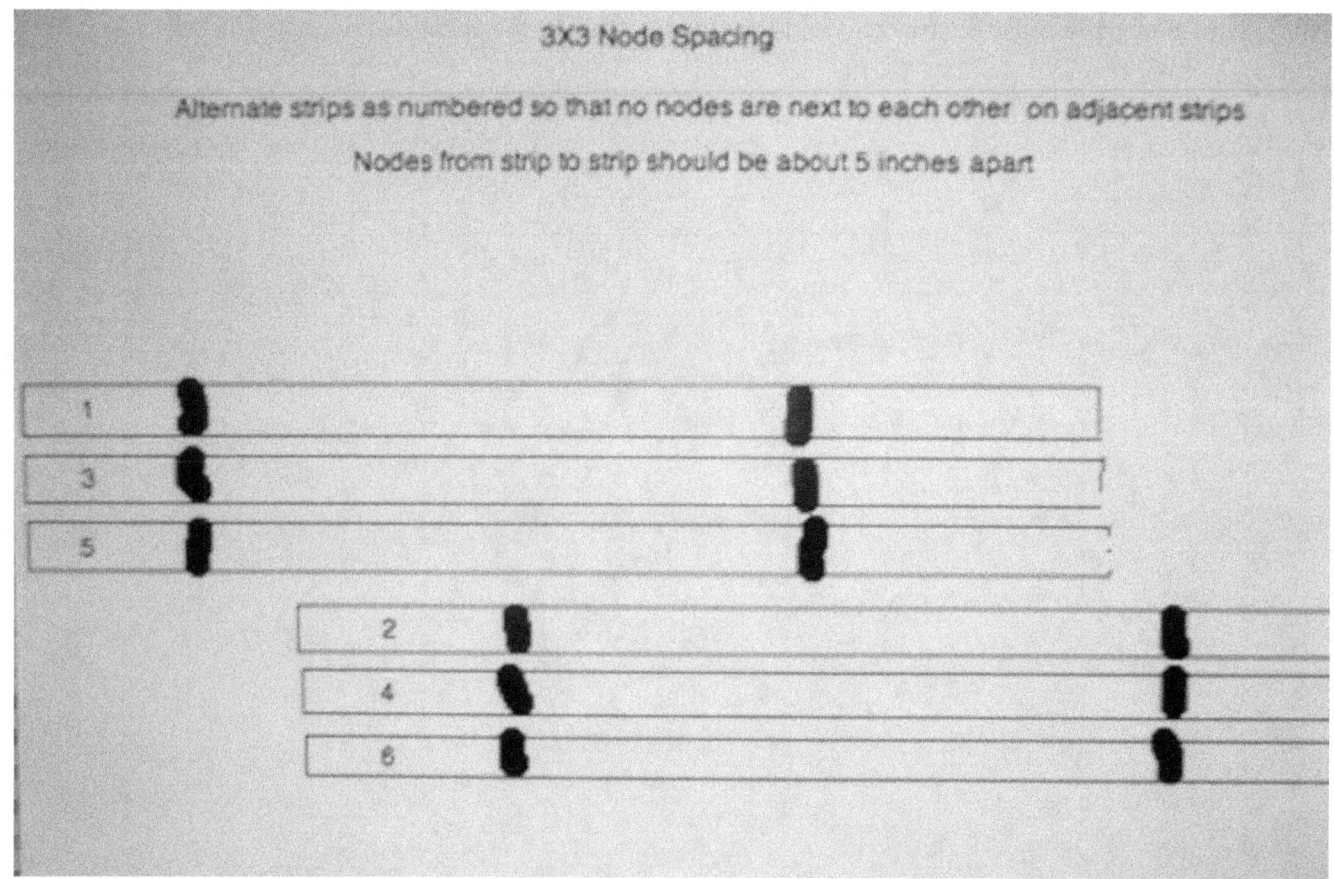

Figure 5.2: 3x3 node spacing

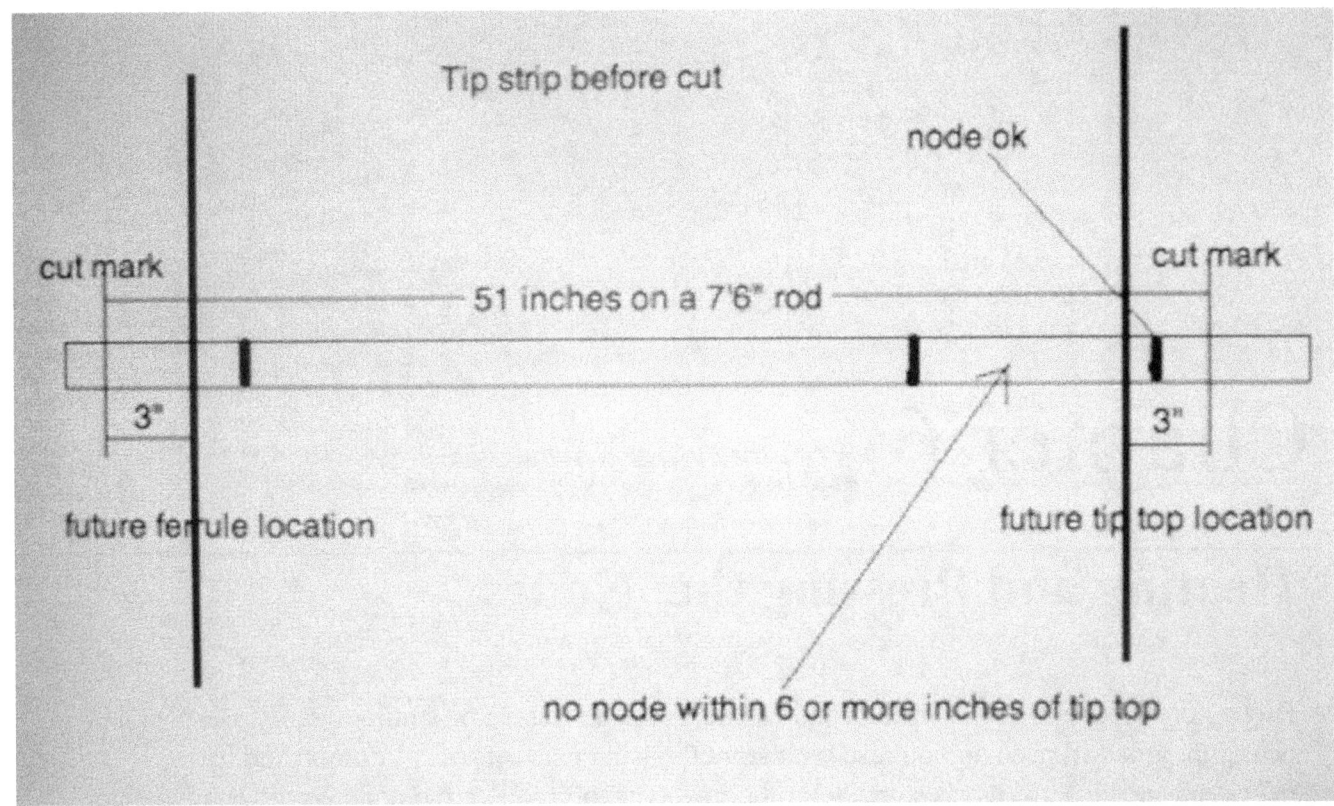

Figure 5.3: 3x3 node spacing

Chapter 6

Heating and Pressing the Nodes

Buy a good heat gun such as Black and Decker, Bosch, Wagner or similar quality. Besides the heat gun, you will need a good vise with smooth jaws measuring 4". I do not find it necessary to file a groove as some do in the jaw to accommodate the node on the enamel side. I mounted my heat gun on some plywood so that it sits on the bench and blows air up vertically. Fig. 6.1. You will want to use both hands to hold the strip while heating and later when straightening. Take a scrap piece of strip that you cut off earlier and practice heating it up at the node. You want to pass the strip back and forth over the heat gun and also rotating it at the same time until it heats up enough that the cane softens somewhat. A fan style attachment on the gun is handy. If you are making a blonde rod avoid heating the enamel side so that it won't darken. The pith side will char a bit and this is fine. Just get the sides of the strip to darken a bit without charring them. You will notice that the butt strips will have more nodes and are thicker than the tip strips, so they will require more patience. Now place the heated strip into the nearby vise and really clamp down on it. If you have done this properly there will be a give (compression) when the vise is tightened on the node. By the time you heat your next strip the one in the vise will have cooled enough for removal. You will have fun taking one out and placing another in the vise in a quick fashion. How well can you juggle?

Practice on a couple of more practice strips and then start on your real strips. Thank God that's over until the next rod. (Obviously, heating and pressing nodes is not my favorite process). Keep in mind though, that you may have to do some more in case you break a strip later during the process.

Figure 6.1: Heating nodes with a heat gun

Figure 6.2: Pressing nodes

Chapter 7

Plane Selection

All right! We're moving along and it's time to plane some cane. We're going to be real artisans like those old guys who hang out in the shops in their basements with their glasses sliding down their noses.

What plane should I buy? Books and forums say to get a Stanley for rough planing. Others say make sure to get a Lie Nielsen rod maker's plane because of the grove. Others say buy a Veritas.
Can't beat them. This is what I say. Mr. Stanley is made for the weekender do it yourselfers. I bought one when I started out making rods because, after all, it was the thing to do, or so I thought. Hell, I had spent months reading books and skimming through the forums. I even sucked in for the training wheels that can be put on them. They can be seen if you poke around on the Internet, or have a copy of The Best of the Planing Form (a good book for the most part). The only enjoyment that plane gave me was when I painted it up really fancy. I think that I made it red and black and even put some eyeballs on it. Turns out that I sold it on the eBay for a great price. Perhaps I should have kept it. Here is the real deal. If you buy a Stanley you get to spend a few hours moving it across some various grades of sandpaper placed on a flat piece of glass until the bottom is true. Who makes a plane with a bottom that is not perfectly flat? The answer is a company that sells to the average homeowner who does wood working projects on the weekend. Another negative issue that I have with their plane is that the blade quality is poor. Full of chromium so that when Joe Six Pack hangs it on the wall in his garage, it won't rust. The blade won't hold an edge for long because of the chromium. The result is that you spend $45 for the plane, you have found a piece of glass and bought several dollars worth of sand paper and then realize that you have to buy a Hock (wonderful

company) blade for around $50 or more. You now have over a hundred bucks invested plus labor involved in the plane that those great rod builders told you to get and then find out that adjusting the blade is a pain in the ass and it is a clumsy, especially for a beginner. Here is what to do. It is important and you will thank me for the tip. Buy a Lie Nielsen #103 standard 20° angle block plane. Spend a little more and get a second
sucked in for the training wheels that can be put on them. They can be seen if you poke around on the Internet, or have a copy of The Best of the Planing Form (a good book for the most part).

Here is the real deal. If you buy a Stanley you get to spend a few hours moving it across some various grades of sandpaper placed on a flat piece of glass until the bottom is true. Who makes a plane with a bottom that is not perfectly flat? The answer is a company that sells to the average homeowner who does wood working projects on the weekend. Another negative issue that I have with their plane is that the blade quality is poor. Full of chromium so that when Joe Six Pack hangs it on the wall in his garage, it won't rust. The blade won't hold an edge for long because of the chromium. The result is that you spend $45 for the plane, you have found a piece of glass and bought several dollars worth of sand paper and then realize that you have to buy a Hock (wonderful company) blade for around $50 or more. You now have over a hundred bucks invested plus labor involved in the plane that those great rod builders told you to get and then find out that adjusting the blade is a pain in the ass and it is a clumsy, especially for a beginner. Here is what to do. It is important and you will thank me for the tip. Buy a Lie Nielsen #103 standard 20° angle block plane. Spend a little more and get a second plane. A Lie Nielsen adjustable, for rough planing and use the Lie Neilson #103 for secondary and final planing. Both planes already have a flat bottom, and a great blade, and move along the bamboo like a Ferrari.

During rough planing, I bent a couple of brass blade hold down wheels on my Lie Nielsen #103. I am an aggressive planer when I rough plane strips. Lie Nielsen guarantees their parts for life so they sent me a couple of wheels, and as I remember, they even picked up the freight. In my opinion there is no better plane at the price. I have noticed, however, that on the Lie Nielsen #103, the blade placement relative to the throat opening can vary from plane to plane. In some of them, the blade orientation is a bit too close to the front of the opening, which causes a problem. It is easily remedied by carefully widening the front of that throat opening with a flat jeweler's file, as you will need it later anyway when you prepare your ferrules before wrapping.

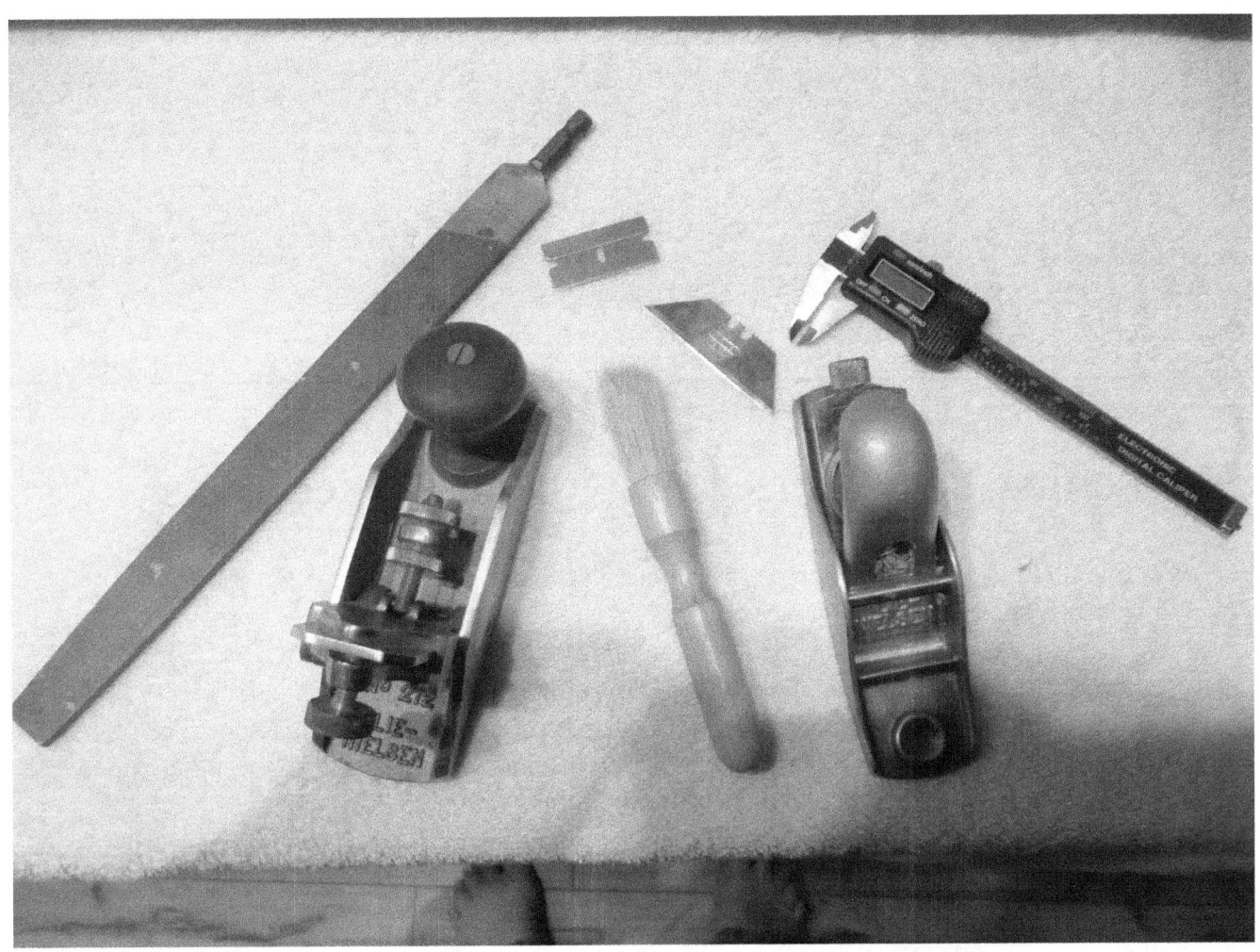

Figure 7.1: Tools used in planing strips

Chapter 8

Sharpening Your Plane Iron with the Proper Tools

You will find all kinds of information on the proper way to sharpen.
I will give this suggestion, which was given to me by the guy who sold me those crazy training wheels for the Stanley block plane. There are machines out there that have elaborate jigs and various wheels that sell for about $500. I was thinking about buying one until I received a new blade from a supplier who had pre-sharpened my iron using a machine like this. The blade was fairly sharp, but not sharp enough for our type of work. I suggest that you buy a diamond stone made by DMT. (Fig 8.1) Don't buy the one with the interrupted surface (looks like a cheese grader). Make sure to get a fine grit and an extra fine The 600 and 1500 grit in a large enough size for instance, 2½" × 11" or 3" × 8". The stone can be cleaned periodically using a Scotch Brite pad and Comet Cleanser.

You will also need a Japanese water stone. I like one with 8,000 grit. Make sure it has Japanese writing on its box and that it comes with a Nagura stone. This included stone is used for truing the water stone after several uses. After a lot of use, it can be flattened using 60 grit sandpaper placed on a flat piece of glass.

You will need a device to hold your blade when sharpening. I like the Veritas jig system. It can be bought as a set from Highland Hardware and others. Use the angle set to 30° to hold your plane blade. It is most often suggested to sharpen the blade at 30°. This is fine, but I found out purely by accident that my plane performs better at a steeper angle, especially during final planing. Sometimes the blade tends to submarine into the bamboo when sharpened to 30°. This became quite annoying, especially when it ruined a strip. When you sharpen, start out at 30°. As the blade dulls, don't spend the time to grind all of its surface back to 30°. Instead, slightly increase the blade's angle into the jig, that way you will sharpen faster and get better performance. The Veritas jig has a feature that allows you to slightly increase the angle without removing the blade. You only need about a 32nd" or so of the edge sharpened. When you have finished preparing the blade on the diamond stone, take the blade (still in the jig) over to the water stone, which should have been soaking in a shallow baking dish for about 15 minutes. This step will polish the blade and put a good edge on it. I flip the jig over with the blade still in it and run it across the water stone. This takes off any minute burrs, much as the old barber's leather strap did. Note: When sharpening on the diamond stone, turn the blade jig 180 and rub it across the DMT several times to take off any burrs on the backside of the blade.

41

Take the blade (still in the jig) over to the water stone, which should have been soaking in a shallow baking dish for about 15 minutes. This step will polish the blade and put a good edge on it. I flip the jig over with the blade still in it and run it across the water stone. This takes off any minute burrs, much as the old barber's leather strap did. Note: When sharpening on the diamond stone, turn the blade jig 180 and rub it across the DMT several times to take off any burrs on the backside of the blade.When you have the blade properly sharpened, it will make a noticeably friendly sound as it slides down the bamboo strip. It should not grab at all. During rough planing you don't have to be that fussy on the sharpening. You are just hogging off material. Do, however, pay special attention to sharpening while secondary, and especially during final planing. I will discuss how often to sharpen in the segment covering final planing.

When the blade's angle gets too high it is time to bring it back to 30°. I bought a Work

Fig 8.1.: Diamond stone & water stone showing Veritas jig

Sharp blade grinder Dip the blade into a cup of water periodically to cool it off as you continue putting the blade into the Work Sharp which will have a setting for a 30-degree angle.

Chapter 9
Rough Planing

Rough planing provides a good exercise for getting used to how the plane will work on the bamboo. You should consider working on a test strip. After a while you will become familiar with how to hold the plane, keeping it level and, also how much pressure to apply.
I rough plane in a variety of places. I use my workbench, kitchen table and sometimes the top of my table saw. Recently I took a seven-foot 2x12 and placed it on telescoping stands at each end. This set up allows for planing in either direction and on either side of the 2x12 depending on whether you prefer right hand or left hand operation.
I also use a ratchet clamp to hold the piece. (Chapter 10 Fig. 10.1.
Beware ... bamboo is extremely sharp and can cut the heck out of you if it slips through your hand while planing. I have cut myself many times and it is not fun. I began to use gloves after my first bloodletting, but I think eventually that you will put the gloves aside. Gloves interfere with the dexterity required to make a rod. The tighter fitting gloves available make your hands sweat.
I have built bevelers and have used commercially built ones. I have decided to stay away from them. I came to the conclusion that I can rough plane strips by hand as fast as I can crank them out on a beveler. Perhaps I am the exception. Who knows, who cares? If you hate rough planing or hogging as I call it, you can look at the Little Giant beveler on the Bellinger web site. Another nice one is the Quinchat, or what is known as the Bertram Multi Track.

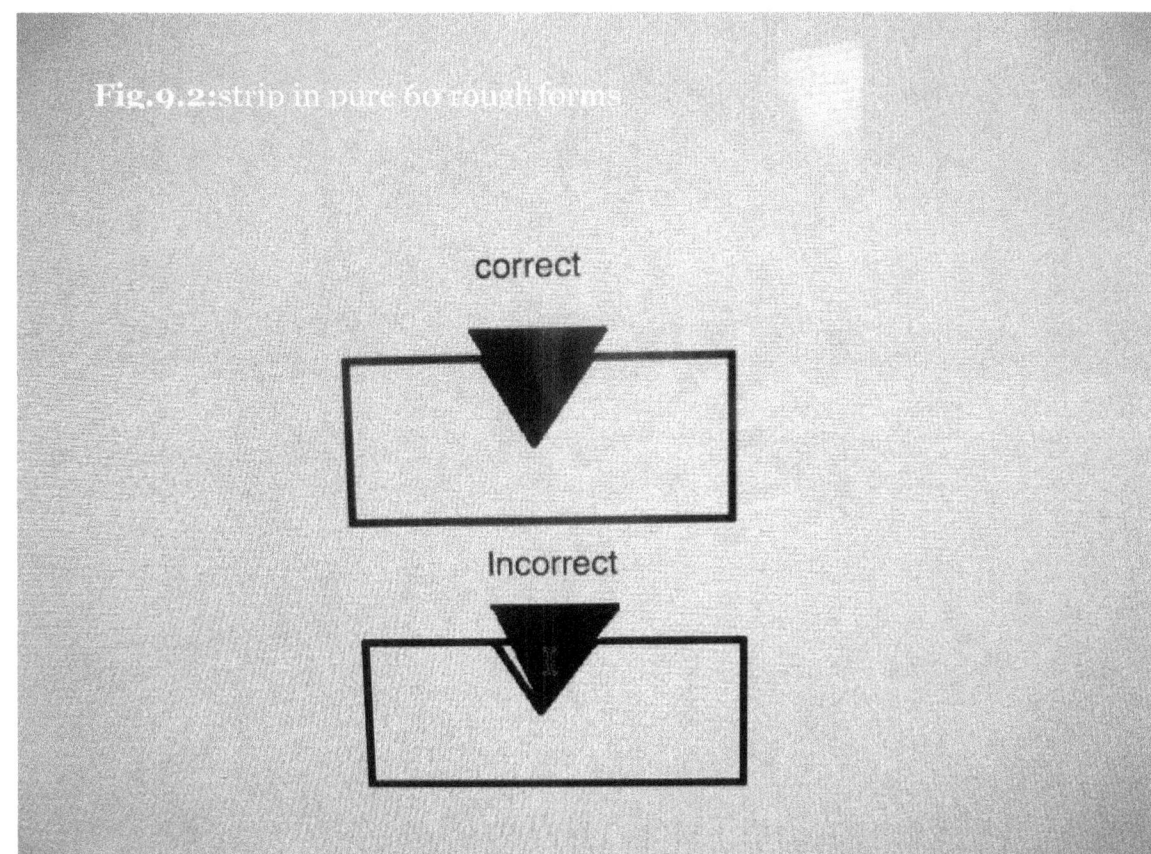

Fig.9.2: strip in pure 60 rough forms

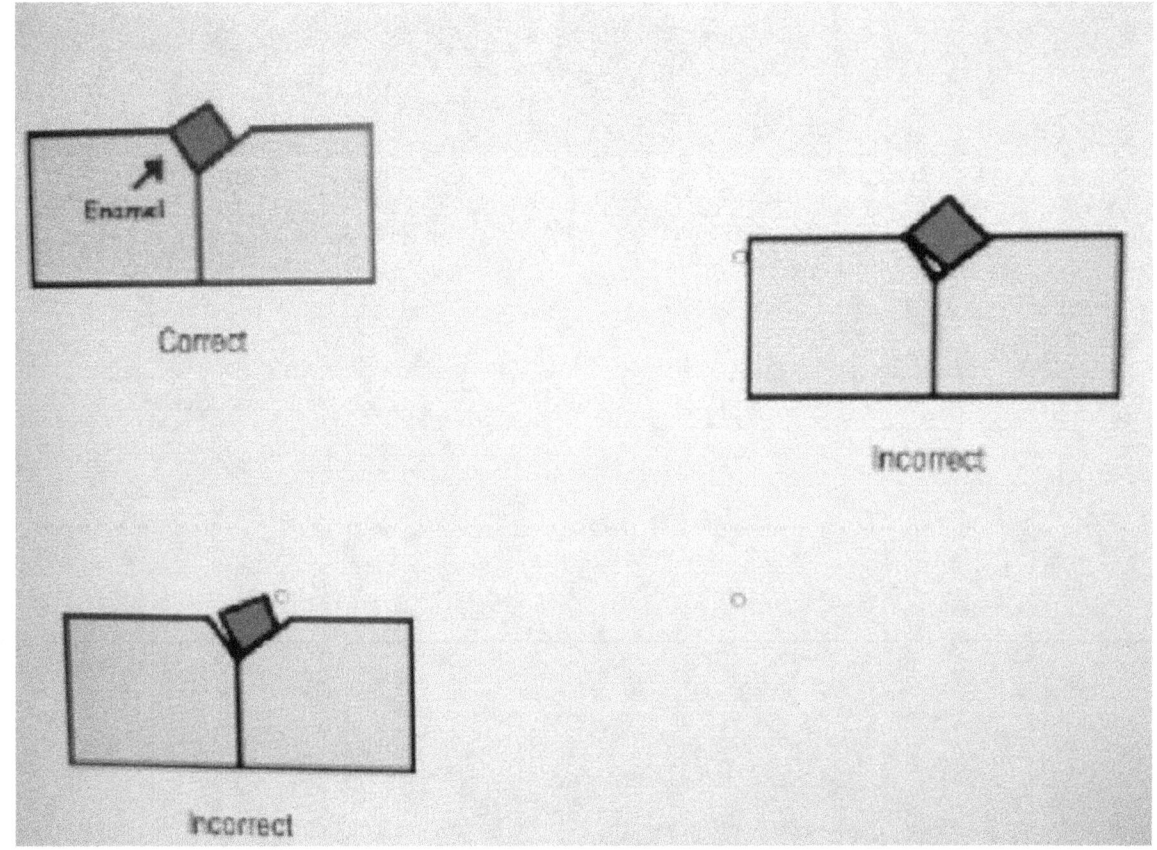

Figure 9.4: Periodically checking the angle of a strip using a center gauge

Chapter 10

Rough Planing Forms

The rough form can be made or bought. I buy mine from Jeff Wagner for about $40. The form has one side grooved (shallow grooves) for tips and the other side grooved for butts (deeper grooves). On each side, one groove is a perfect 60° angle and the other has a 30° wall and then a 57° wall. There are disagreements among some builders about having the 57° angles. Some like to have a 58° and others use a 52°. The 57° works for me, and produces a good final 60° angle.

The forms are constructed in such a way as to end up with the proper height of the strips being produced. That is to say the depths of the butt and tip sides of the forms yield the correct size of strip. Rough plane your finished strips to be slightly above the surface of your form. That way you will not beat up the form by planing into it. If you should build your own forms, the butt grove should be about ¼" deep and the tip grove depth should be about ⅛" deep.

The important thing is to get the strips to fit nicely into the rough form. If the strips have some bad bends heat them up with your heat gun until the bamboo softens slightly and then apply pressure to force the bend to become straight. This may have to be repeated a few times to take the bend out.

Before rough planing, you must address the enamel side of the node. It will not fit into the form properly if the enamel side of the node is not relatively flat. A beginner will find the nodes are most easily dressed using a bastard file. I now use the circular wheel on my belt sander, but caution must be used not to dig into the power fibers next to the nodal area.

Figure 10.1: Using the roughing form

I recommend that you start with the file to get the main bumps off the node. It does not have to be perfectly smooth or dressed until later. Now that the strip is relatively straight and the node is reasonably flat place the strip flat on a table enamel side down and plane off the burnt portion of the node on pith side. Blend this area in over about 3 or 4 inches so the area is flat with no bumps present.

Start the planing with the 57 ° and 30°angled grooves. Make certain that the enamel side is firmly placed against the 30° high angled side of that groove. To get perfect 60° angles the strip must be well placed against that wall. The strip must be checked during this process to always make sure that the strip is fitting properly into the form. Check this often by looking at the strip at the very end of the form. Fig. 10.4 and 10.5.

The strip can be clamped in this position or you start at one end without using a clamp until you get about 4" or 5" started. You will notice that as you progress, a 60° angle is being created on one side of the strip. Caution! Never plane the enamel side of the strip! I take off quite a thick curl when I rough plane because I am eager to move along and after all you are just hogging wood. You should frequently use a center gauge to check your angle. Fig.10.3.This item can be bought at most machine shop supply houses with various sized 60° angles cut into its edges. Keep track of it. Paint it red if necessary. I have had to buy a few because I have accidentally thrown some out that dropped into the shavings.

10.1 Helpful Tricks

I made some short 26" to 28" long forms with only the 30° and 57° angles. I made one with a deep cut for butt strips and one with a shallower cut for tip strips ¼ and ⅛ respectively. This short form allows you to work on a smaller section of the strip and lets the remainder of the strip overhang on the form. Work down the strip moving it in the short form. The advantage here is that the irregularities in the strip won't sit in the long form causing it to rock out of position. Sometimes the side of the strip that you are working on still will not have a perfect 60° angle when checked with the center gauge, as shown in Fig. 10.3. To remedy this, rotate the form 180° and work on the side that was not planed. The side you have newly planed will now fit better into the form because the irregularities on the side you first planed have been removed. You should find that the new side worked on would have a more accurate 60° angle. Place this newly worked side down into the 60° grooves on the longer form.

If your tip strips are a bit wide and rock in the shallow form when trying to establish your first 60° angle, check to see if they will fit into the deeper butt side of the form. This deeper form with a higher wall will better support the strip.

If the strip does not fit into the form correctly follow these steps.

1. If the strip does not fit well into the grove, flip the form 180° and try putting the strip into the form from the other direction.

Figure 10.2: Using the roughing form

2. If this does not help remove the strip and plane some material off the sides of the strip freehand. The strip must be checked during this process to always make sure that the strip is fitting properly into the form. Make no big bend in the strip exists and that it is not twisted from one end to the other. Use a heat gun to correct these problems.

3. After one side now has the 60° angles you can place that side into the pure 60° grooves on the form and begin to plane the other pith side. Just make certain that you have good 60° angles being formed and that you are removing the same amount of material from both sides. This is one of the critical steps in producing an outstanding fly rod. Frequently check the ends of the strips to make sure that they are fitting into the forms as pictured in figures 10.4 and 10.5, below. When looking at both ends of the strip you should see a good equilateral triangle. If it is just a bit off, don't worry. It will be corrected when the metal form is used in a later step. Periodically look at the strip right at the end of the form to check the angle.

For Notes

Chapter 11
Binders and Binding before Heat Treating

There are various binders that can be used when building a bamboo fly rod. Simply put, the binder is a device that clamps the bamboo strips together before heat-treating, or during the gluing process. We want a binder that is simple to use, will efficiently hold the pieces together, is reliable and will minimize twisting during the gluing process. I will purposely stay away from comparing equipment and differences in methods in this regard.

The clamping is achieved by tightly wrapped string that follows a fairly close crosshatch pattern over the length of the rod. The rod section is run through the binder twice to accomplish this. The string used is usually glaced cotton size 16/4. The rod is driven through the binder by a looped or continuous drive belt. The belt material is either Dacron or nylon string. The belt can be hand cranked or driven by a variable speed drill. I happen to like the binder sold by Jeff Wagner. I will recommend other products of his from time to time.

Jeff is a first class rod builder who has years of experience, however the thing that I like about him the most is that he is a no bullshit kind of guy. He does what he does because he loves it. He has been a straight shooter with me and has always been there to answer questions, giving me honest, accurate and sensible answers. He realizes, as I do, that if you want to become an icon in this field, your work must speak for itself, and you must always be willing to help and encourage others. Jeff's binder is diagramed in my appendix.

Making your own tools sometimes makes sense or it can be just plain fun. In most cases, it is more practical to buy your tools. The strips have been rough planed and you are happy with the 60° angles. You are ready to bind them together. You are not expected to build an award winning bamboo fly rod at this point. You want to make your own bamboo fly rod that will look good, cast well and will catch fish. If you get hooked on this craft, there is plenty of time to improve your skills. My job is to keep your first attempt from going into the wood stove.

11.1 Getting Ready To Heat Treat

Lay your strips out on a table and place the enamel side down. Separate the strips into two groups. Because you have used the 3 × 3 node spacing method, you have 3 strips that are alike

with respect to their node location, and another set of three strips that are also alike. Put down some ¾" masking tape on your table sticky side up. Cut the length of the tape at about 2". Now place a strip from one of the groups with the first node furthest toward the end marked black (remember the marks you put on the ends before you split the cane) these marked ends should all be on your left. As close as possible, place the next strip from the other group of three next to the first strip. Continue this process until all strips are next to each other on the table with the enamel down and stuck to the tape with the apex of the triangle facing up. Cut the excess tape that shows at the top of the strips with a razor blade close to the first strip that you put down. Lift the strips off from the table and roll them together forming a hexagon blank. The black marked ends at your left should be together. Tear off another piece of tape and wrap it around at the mid point of the strips. Press the strips together there. Place a third piece of tape down towards the end of the strips. It is best to have the first and last piece of tape about three or four inches away from each end. This will make things easier when you run the strips through the binder.

Figure 11.1: Above

11.2 Using the Binder X-ing Pattern

The first use of the binder will effectively clamp the strips together before heat-treating. You will notice that since the strips are not exactly the same size at this point, they may not move through the binder smoothly. The section may stop or even cut the thread on the first trip through. Just give them some coaxing using your fingers to aid them through. I make it a practice to send the butts through first with the marked ends at the left. I do the tips exactly opposite sending the marked ends through first. Another way to say this is "send the ferrule ends through first". There will be more on this when binding the strips while gluing. I like to attach my variable speed power drill to the Wagner style binder. It makes for a consistent and a fast run through. Lay the taped strips into the binder and wind the drive belt around the strips as shown in fig.11.2.Tie on the string using half hitches as shown. Start to run the strips through stopping to remove the tape before the string goes around the blank and covers that tape. I wrap the drive belt around the blank away from me for the first pass through and then towards me before the second pass. This accomplishes the crosshatch pattern.

Here is the sequence of tying on the drive belt and string to achieve the X-ing pattern.

Figure 11.2: Using the binder and attaching the drive string and clamping string

Figure 11.3: Using the binder first pass

Fig. 11.4.:Establishing the X ing or cross hatch

Chapter 12

Heat Treating Methods. A Simple Oven and Some Options

When I started out, I did not want to spend a lot of money on an oven. I saw one on the Internet for about $800. Wow!

There are three basic types of heat-treating ovens.

Method 1: Uses a heat gun and stovepipe, but I would recommend you avoid this technique.

Method 2: Uses copper pipe and a propane torch. I made at least 50 rods using this technique. It does a fine job, and in some ways, I like it better than the electric oven.

Method 3: Is a heat strip style oven, which I use exclusively today. Plans, along with where to get the heat strip, thermostat and box are provided in the appendix of this book.

12.1 Constructing a Copper Pipe Oven

While searching around the Internet I ran across a German rod maker who was using a copper pipe placed inside of a second copper pipe. He heated the outer pipe using a propane torch. It sounded kind of primitive and I was worried burning strips using this technique. Once I got the hang of it, the device was turning out very good results. I decided to make two units, one for tips and one for butts. If I built only one to use for both sections I would be spending too much time heating the tip section in the tube that was large enough to accommodate the butt section.

The pipe for the tip section consists of a ¾" copper outer pipe and then a ½" copper pipe placed inside of it. This provides an air space between the two. Standard copper plumbing pipe was used. The length of my pipe is 64" for both tip and butt sections. This length will accommodate about any two-piece rod that you want to make. Solder on some scrap copper between the two pipes to create an air space between the two pipes.

You do not want the strips to come in contact directly with the outer tube when it is being heated. Lead based solder has a rather low melting point and can melt when you heat the pipe with the torch. I found that non-lead solder, which has a higher melting temperature, solved this problem. Drill two, 1/16" holes that go through both pipes at about 4" from each end. When the strips get to the proper temperature and begin to cook, you will notice steam escaping from these holes. Check the holes periodically with a toothpick to make sure you have a clear path for steam to escape. I found a way to mount temperature gauges at each end. I used ¾" male adapters (don't solder to the pipe) that accommodated the gauges that I bought at a hardware store. The interior of the threaded end of the adaptors can be tapped out so the thermometer can be threaded into them. The thermometer assemblies can be removed at either end when I want to insert strips or transfer the thermometers to the larger butt pipe.

12.1 Note on Building the Butt Pipe

I constructed the butt pipe the same length as the tip pipe. I used 1¼" copper for the outer pipe and 1" copper for the inner pipe. It turns out that 1" copper couplings make perfect spacers.

Solder 3 onto the 1" inner pipe. Extend the one-inch pipe beyond the outer pipe so that you can solder on fittings. At one end solder on a 1" coupling and then solder into that a 1" by ¾" slip by slip reduces bushing. Inside of that solder in a short piece of ¾" copper pipe so that the temperature gauge unit will fit onto it. This obviously will not be soldered on. This will not be the end that the strips will go into because they won't fit into this end. At the other end of the pipe you should have the 1" inner pipe extending beyond the 1¼" outer pipe. Here you use a one inch coupling which will have a 1" by ¾" slip-by-slip reducing bushing soldered into it. Into that, solder in a short piece of ¾" pipe so that you can slip the second temperature gauge on it. This completed fitting is not soldered on to the end of the inner tube. It must be removable so that you can slide the butt blank into this end.

Figure 12.1: Making the tube-The copper pipes

Fig.12.2: A student uses the pipe method

Fig.12.3 Hanging the pipe heater

60

12.1 Using the Copper Pipe Oven

I use my BernzOmatic TS4000 to heat the pipe at its bottom. I suspend the pipe from the ceiling using swag light hooks and chain. The pipe is held through the bottom of the chains with some thick copper wire fashioned so that you can rotate the pipe while heating. First, heat the pipe without the strips in it. Protect your hand to avoid getting burned. Make sure the end caps are on the pipe. I heat the tube to about 280 before placing the bound strips inside the tube. Make sure you sight down the bound blank and get it as straight as possible before placing it in the pipe. I roll the blank on a flat table much as you would roll out dough. You can then tweak the blank from side to side while you sight down it. It will

bend easily before it is heat-treated. When both gauges read from 260°F to 300°F, insert the strips at one end by removing the gauge unit. Slide the blank into the pipe and give it a bit of a push. Fire up the torch and heat the tube from the bottom only. Travel the torch from one end to the other while rotating the pipe about ¼ turn at a time. Keep the temperature reading on the gauges between 280 to 300°F, no more. After about 8 to 10 minutes you will notice the steam exiting the two holes. Sometimes I have to give the pipe a good shake to get the steam coming out at both holes because the blank inside may be blocking one of the holes. All culms differ in moisture content, so there is no exact time that can be specified to cook tips and butts. As a general rule, I cook tips for about 20 minutes and butts for about 25 minutes. You must get used to this method and keep your eye on the steam escaping from the two holes. When the steam starts decreasing and finally stops coming out of the holes it is your signal that the blank has been cooked. On your first attempt you will be nervous about burning the strips so you might undercook the section a little. You don't, however want to over cook. This will be identified if the strips are quite dark on the pith side when unwrapped. This results in difficulty planing and perhaps a brittle rod due to weakened power fibers. I know that this technique sounds crude, but it works.

Remove the cooked blank from the tube using a hot pad and by lowering one end and shaking the pipe downward in this process. Set it aside on a flat surface to cool. Once cooled, make sure that when you bend the blank from side to side it springs back nicely and does not set as it did before you cooked it. If it does set, you have under cooked the section and need to heat it up for another ten minutes.

12.2 An Electric Oven

Plans and more pictures for this electric oven can be found in the appendix.

Figure 12.4: Electric oven

The electric oven uses a 120 VAC heating strip and it is controlled by a thermostat similar to those found in household ovens. It consists of two rectangular sheet metal boxes with boiler grade insulation in between. The rod sections are placed on top of rat wire. It's easy to use and is faster than the pipe ovens.

An approximate cooking time at 375°F is 34 minutes for tips and 38 minutes for butts. The sections should be taken out and switched end-to-end 180° after cooking ½ these times. The tip section and butt sections are done separately.

Chapter 13 The Metal Planing Form

I consider the metal planing form to rank as the most important tool you will buy and use in the rod making process. I can't over emphasize that you should not skimp on this tool. A quality form will make the difference between producing a quality rod or just a mediocre one. I was very tempted to save some money and buy a less expensive form, but luckily I did not. You will see forms selling from about $350 to over a thousand dollars. Their construction is not as simple as you would imagine. It is not just a matter of finding a machine shop (even if it is a good one) that uses some cold rolled steel and cranks one out from some plans that you give him. The machine shop must be familiar with the process of making a form and must have made many of them. There is a lot of truing and special grinding involved in making a form that will be accurate to one thousandth of an inch. I have known rod makers who settled for less than the best, and were unhappy when the final numbers on a strip were checked with a caliper. The numbers could be off as much as 0.005 on such a form. This amount will not only significantly change the behavior of the rod, but will frustrate you by adding time consuming steps to correct the problem.

I bought my form from Jeff Wagner as several rod makers told me his was the best form available and the numbers were right on target when the plane blade reached the top of the form. They were right. I now own two of his forms and could not be more pleased. Jeff can also supply the dial gauge used to set the stations, but most importantly, he will supply a standard with a 60° grove in it. This standard is important to properly calibrate the dial gauge. Many form suppliers will tell you to calibrate the dial gauge on a flat surface. This is just a falsehood, trust me.

I happen to really like building rods with swelled butts so I spent a little more for his swelled butt form. This is a matter of choice. Jeff's swelled butt form has a noticeable groove machined into the form that makes for a well-shaped swell. Other forms just open wider at the swell, but don't have the machined groove.

64

Figure 13.1: Machined swell in form

If you do buy the form from Jeff, you will get a set of instructions on how to use it. He will be glad to answer your questions if anything is unclear. Therefore, I will not get into a detailed discussion of the mechanics of how the form works. Simply put, the form is designed on the principle of a push pull system using two bolts for adjustment with a dowel pin between them. One bolt pushes the form apart and the other pulls the form together. His form is simple to adjust because it has all of the adjustment bolts on one side of the form with dowel pins centered between them. These are spaced over the length of the form every 5 inches.

13.1 Using Your Form before Planing Begins

Set up the form per the instructions included. Make sure to calibrate your dial gauge using a standard. If you are using a form from another supplier, make sure that you buy and use a standard. Without one, I guarantee your measurements will be off! After the form is set up and you select the desired taper you want, start working on the tip section first. One side of the form is designed to hold the tips and the other holds the butts. On my form, when the adjustment screws face you, the first station, (smallest setting dimension) sometimes called the zero station, is located as the last one on your right. This will be your first station taper measurement and will be the location of your tip top. Some rod makers place masking tape on the table or on the side of the form where they mark the dimension number of each station. These marks will be every five inches going from right to left up the form as the taper dimension increases. I have found it most efficient to mark red lines using a sharpie marker and ruler straight edge on the topside of the form. On my form, the marks up and down the form correspond to the dowel located between the adjustments.

Figure 13.2: A dial gauge is used to set form to taper depth

In any case, they must be exactly 5" apart going up the form. I also mark down the dimension numbers near those lines. Sometimes you have to darken these notations as they wear during final planing. I remove the marks when needed with some 0000 steel wool and Goof Off and then wipe with a paper towel. After making a few rods, widen the form to clean out shavings and debris.

The tip section will be the standard for the length of your rod. The butt will be adjusted in length, if necessary, when the reel seat is attached during the final rod building process. In order to get the measurement (total length) of the tip correct, we will use the 7½' rod as an example. Since the rod will have a total length of 90" it would be assumed that each section would be exactly 45" long. Not true. We must allow for the distance of the ferrules once the rod is put together. You allow for this by making each section a bit longer than 45". This turns out to be a measurement, which is one half longer than the amount of the distance that the ferrule nests into itself. This is usually about ⅜" added to each rod section. Inserting the caliper into the female ferrule and noting the depth at where the caliper stops can determine the exact amount. Then divide this number in half. Let's assume that one half of this number is ⅜". Now put your tape measure so that it's zero mark is lined up at the first station mark (tip top location) extend the tape up to 45" and continue up the form ⅜" further. Make a mark there and label it cut. After the enamel is removed, this mark should be transferred to the strip. Make sure you mark this spot on the form with each rod that you make. It is important! It indicates where the tip section will be cut before ferruling. The butt section will be done a little differently and discussed later.

13.1 Let's Start Planing

Using a razor blade, remove the string from the heat-treated blank. Cut through the two strings at the ferrule of end blank and remove one string at a time. The blank will spin and separate in the process. Where to I plane? Many times you will be planing in both directions. Depending on your dexterity, it may be hard to do this if you have the metal form on a typical wide workbench. The height of the bench may also be uncomfortable depending on how tall you are. Since I have some issues with my back, I came up with this solution. I use a seven-foot long 2x12 mounted on tripods.

These are often used when cutting long pieces of plywood on a table saw. I removed the rollers and drilled some holes in the vertical shaft so that I can adjust the height to suit different people. The telescoping feature on my device failed by slipping. This arrangement can also be used for rough planing. Fig.13.3

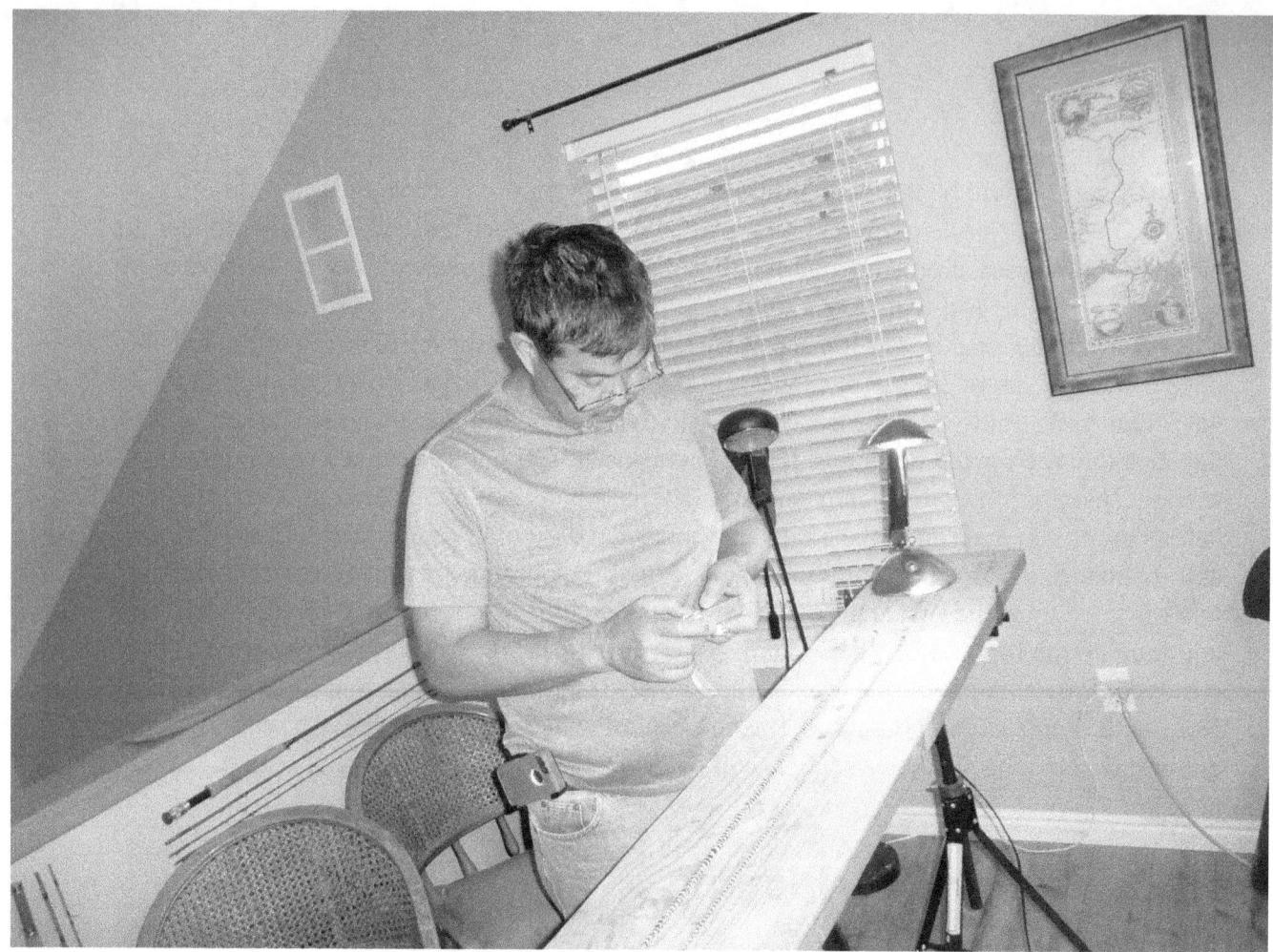

Figure 13.3: My planing table

Begin with the tip strips.
Place the strips up on the bench near your metal form with the red marked ends to your left. This will represent the ferrule end of the tip section. Always make sure the strip enters the form with the red marked end on the left or at the widest form setting. They can get mixed up when you are scraping off the enamel in a later step. Ensure your plane blade is sharp before you start plaining. Set the plane blade so the curls coming off the material measure between

0.003" to 0.005". You will need to buy an accurate digital caliper to ensure curl thickness. I think a caliper that opens up to 4" and has an overall length of no more than 6½" is best. You are able to take off more material at this stage of planing than you will later on.. There is one smaller tool you will need before planing on the metal form. How do I hold the strip in place on the form so it does not slide? Use a soft pink eraser, like the ones you used in school. If you press down firmly on the eraser, it will hold the strip in place. Sometimes I also use a

Sometimes I also use a spring clamp. Since the strip is much wider now than it will be later you don't want to place it in the form down too far toward the first station. Start planing by placing the strip into the wider section of the form. That is to say a long ways upstream from the smallest station. If the strip is started too far down the form in the narrower portion of the form, it will tend to rock and you will not be able to keep your plane in a horizontal position while planing.

Some rod makers will completely finish one strip at a time as they plane. But I do things a bit differently. I do not finish each strip before moving on to the next strip. This would truly be called final planing.. I use a technique that I picked up from the Garrison book called secondary planning. This made sense to me because it acts as a forced quality control on your work. The principle of secondary planing suggests that you take all of the strips down to within 0.005 to.015", or a little more, above the metal form and then set them aside. I am not saying using the secondary planing technique will completely eliminate all of your problems, but it sure will reduce them. Keep the form clean during planing using a paintbrush. Debris in the groove will raise a strip in the form resulting in too much material being taken off the strip. Since the strips won't be perfectly flat after the rough planing, it will take about 4 passes until the plane moves nicely down the strip. You should make no more than 4 passes on one side of the strip before rotating it so that the other pith side is exposed. After 3 or 4 flips on that portion of the strip you can move the strip down the form so that the portion that you have not planed lies in the same spot as your first portion did. I then plane in the opposite direction to smooth out the un-planed portion of the strip. I have had no difficulty planing in either direction on a strip. Sometimes being able to do this is beneficial when overcoming chips or rough spots. After making several passes down both sides of the strips, it is time to take off the enamel. I am sure you will notice that there are disagreements between rod makers as to when to remove enamel during the process.

Figure 13.4: Starting the second planning using the metal form

70
Some rod makers like to take the enamel off after the blank is glued together. There are a variety of ways to build a fly rod. There is more than one way to skin a cat! I am sure that if you decide to continue building bamboo fly rods, you will adopt new and different techniques suited to your personal comfort.

Chapter 14

Planing tips

Place the strip enamel side up in the form. Find your first node down toward the first station. There can be one below the first station, but remember on tip strips, there should not be a node within several inches up stream of the first station (if you spaced your nodes and cut the strips in the right place). Using a bastard file, (Highland Hardware, Lowes or Home Depot sells a good one) file the node so that it is smooth. Make sure to keep the file parallel to the form surface. Go a little beyond the nodal area so you blend into the adjacent portion of the strip. Be careful not to dig into the power fibers. Now take a good sanding block, I prefer one made out of ¾" pine measuring about 3½" × 1⅜" or so. Wrap some 60 grit 3M sandpaper around it and sand over the area of the node until you cannot detect any bump or rough spot. If there is still a bump, file or sand a little more. If you remember, we did not dress the nodes perfectly before rough planing. We want the nodes to be smooth and blended in with the surrounding area. Have we disturbed any power fibers using this method? Does it really matter? Would that rod cast less well, or hold up less well than a rod that had no power fibers disturbed? There are many discussions on this subject that you can view on the Internet forums or ipublications.

After you have properly dressed the nodes, it is time to scrap off the enamel, using a single edge razor blade, working from ferrule end to the tip. Make even strokes until the cnamel is removed revealing the power fibers. This will reveal the beauty that is part of a finished bamboo rod. It is an easy task and involves removing about one-thousandths of an inch. After the enamel is removed, put a little water on the piece to reveal the beauty. After removing the enamel, place the strip into the form with the enamel side up. Place it so that you have some bamboo overhanging the first tip station and also over hanging the ferrule end at the cut mark.

Use a sharp pencil (I use a white China marker on flamed rods) to make a line on the strip that corresponds with your red lines on the form. Include the cut line mark. Mark

these carefully because they will become registration marks that must be at the same place on all of the strips. They will also show where the strip must lie on the form so that you do not plane beyond them in the final planing process. The lines will be used later after the blank has been glued.

You can now place the strip back into the form for further planing. Place the strip way up stream from your bottom tip station. Work on planing one side at a time flipping to the other side after 3 or 4 passes. I usually work on about half of the strip at a time. During this part of the planing process you will be working the strip down the form towards the tip station (smallest measurement) until your marks on the enamel side are just above all the station marks. Once you have completed one strip start on another. You will notice a taper starting to appear. After the enamel has been removed on the next strip take the first strip that you planed and place it in the form enamel side up so that all of its marks correspond to the red lines on the planing form. Now mark the strip you are working so that the marks align in the same place as they are on the first finished strip as the two lay next to each other. Continue this process until all strips have been secondary planed.

14.1 Final Planing

Before beginning final planing, you re-check all of the numbers on the form as they can drift on you, especially when the temperature varies. Pay special attention to sharpening before final planing. It is critical that during final planing, the plane blade is as sharp as it can be. Also it will be helpful that the angle on the plane blade has increased as you have sharpened. You should notice a dramatic difference in the way the plane behaves with this steeper angle and using a well-sharpened blade. It is also important you concentrate. If you are fatigued, you tend to want to complete one more strip when you shouldn't. You also may neglect to sharpen the plane blade when it needs it. Other times you just start screwing up due to fatigue and then you break a strip, or you falsely believe that the strip is close enough to the final measurements. Take the time to make the strips exactly what the taper numbers are.

Finish all tip strips before turning the planning form over to start on the butt strips. You will be changing the form dimensions at that time. Use your dial gauge to check all stations again to make certain that they show the proper taper numbers. Before you do this, place the dial gauge into the standard and make sure that it is calibrated correctly. Take the blade out of the plane and do your best job of sharpening. If the blade is sharpened properly, it will make a clean sounding noise as it glides down the strip. There should be no catching or jumping while planing.

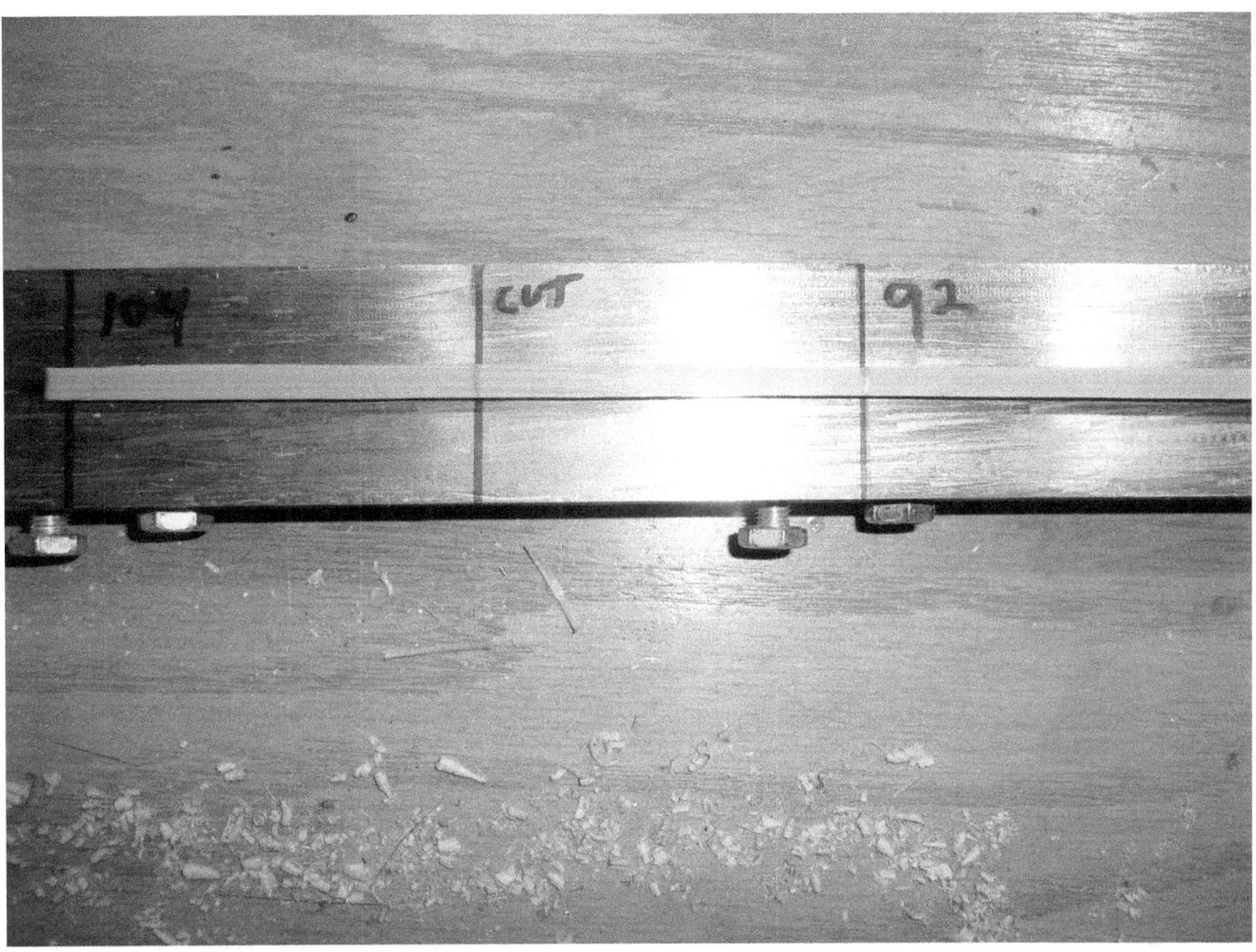

Figure 14.1: Mark strips on enamel side at each station and at cut marks

After the blade is sharp, adjust the blade so it takes off a shaving less than 0.001". Check the curls with your caliper. During final planing hold the plane slightly to the left or right going down the strip. In other words the sides of the plane will not be parallel to the edges of the metal form. Let the plane do the work and don't force the plane by adding more downward pressure. You will now be planing the strips while their marks are just slightly above the station marks on the form. i.e. the strips will be a little oversized.

I have found that after making many rods, some bamboo strips tend to plane better and more smoothly than other bamboo. This is especially true if the sections were over heat-treated, however, I think you will find that tip strips are easier to plane than the butts, mainly because you are planing less material.

Be careful with the fragile tip strips because you can easily break one if the plane or the cuff of your shirt catches on the strip on your back, or pick up stroke. Occasionally a tip strip will separate (break) down near the tip end as you work the plane down the bamboo. This just happens so just make another strip from the extra ones you

made while you were first splitting strips. Sometimes you will encounter problems planing at nodal areas. This is commonly called a chipped node. This can even happen at non-nodal areas. If you run into this, stop and refer to the following solutions. If you run into a problem area do not force the issue plane very slowly. It is possible that the strip will break or you will dig, or as I call it, submarine into the strip. This results in the creating uneven edges, which will result in glue lines showing in the finished rod.

Remedy for Digging or Chipping in at any area on the strip.

Scrape the problem area using either a Lie Nielsen #212 scraping plane (a good plane to have but is expensive and not mandatory). Or a single edged razor blade. Keep a few boxes of them on hand because they have many uses in rod building. A sharp sheet rock knife blade will also work. They can be re-sharpened and are inexpensive. When you run your finger across the problem area you will notice a bump or very rough spot, that I call a step or divot. Scrape this area until the step or divot is almost gone. If the problem is near the smallest tip section be very careful while scraping so that tip does not break. I have had occasions down in that portion of the tip where I have had to scrap the strip by hand until the final taper number is reached. Not fun, but sometimes necessary.

1. Once you believe that the area has been smoothed with your scraper, sharpen your plane blade and make sure that you have adjusted the blade in so that you are just barely taking off any material. Now try light pressure and slowly glide the plane over the problem area. Ideally run the plane in the direction so that the blade won't snag on the step.

2. If the area still causes problems repeat this process and if the problem continues you will have to scrape that area down to the target numbers by hand. Make sure as you are working the surrounding material with the plane that you avoid that area so that your plane does not catch it again. (Putting a red mark there is helpful).

Figure 14.2: Curls from plane and fine shavings from razor blade

3. As a rule of thumb I usually sharpen after doing two or three tip strips and after two butt strips.

Chapter 15

Planing Butt Strips

Again I use the principle of secondary planing before final planing. The butt strips can cause problems because you are removing more bamboo, therefore, sharpen more often. Some problems while planning butt strips can be a dull blade, the blade can submarine into strip, or you can easily have the taper numbers be under the desired measurement due to over planning. Start checking your taper numbers early with a caliper to avoid this problem. It is, however, better to be a bit under the number than over. The gluing process will grow the dimension when 6 strips are glued together. I am a stickler for getting the tip strips within .001 or .002 at each station once the blank is finished. I consider the tip section to be the most important part of the rod. If the butt section is off the target numbers a bit, it will have minimal effect on the action of the fly rod.

Don't bother to plane near the grip area 3 inches above the swell, towards the cork. This will dull the blade unnecessarily and cause you to have to sharpen more often. I don't care if there are some nicks on the flat edges in this area. The cork will cover it and reel seat, while approximately 3 inches below the reel seat, will be cut off later. Just final plane the area on all butt strips from 3 inches above the swell all the way down to the ferrule location with a sharp blade. I then come back and complete all of the butt strips from 3 inches above the swell. I use the somewhat duller plane blade to accomplish this.

Chapter 16
Preparing The Strips To Be Glued

Once you have completed final planing the tip and butt strips, bring them over to a clean working area. I like to remove a small amount of material from the apex of the butt strips with some sandpaper. I use 60 grit on the same block that I sanded the nodes with earlier. Take off a small amount evenly along the strip, just enough to flatten the apex a bit. The purpose of this is to make sure that the strips nest nicely together by giving a bit of leeway to allow for minimal differences in the measurements of the strips and prevent glue lines. It will also allow for a column of glue to run the length of the section down its center, which will add strength to the section.
Starting with the tip strips, locate the first mark that you put on the enamel side near the ferrule portion of the tip strip. The first mark at the ferrule portion of the strip should have been the one that represented the cut mark. The next one down will be the one representing the largest station near the ferrule end and will be the mark we work with. Using a sharp pencil carefully follow that mark around on both sides so that it shows up on the apex side of the strip.
After marking all the strips at this same place, separate them in two groups of three so the nodes are on the same spot in each group. Take a strip from one group and place it enamel side down on a table on top of a 2 inch piece of masking tape. Now take a strip from the second group and place it right next to the first one on the tape so that the marks on the apex match up perfectly. Continue alternating strips on the tape until all six are in place and the nodes line up in an alternating fashion. Make sure all the strips are next to each other as close as possible with no gaps between them. Cut the tape at the top with a razor blade even with the first or top strip. Lift the strips from the table and pinch them together forming a hexagon and secure the tape around them. Go about half way down the rod keeping the strips together to form your hexagon and secure with another piece of tape. At this point double check to make sure that the nodes are not next to each other on adjacent strips. Now put on the last piece of tape at the tip area preferably just below your station mark there. It is good to have the tape 4 to 6 inches from each end so when you place the blank into the binder you have room to

remove the tape and also room enough to attach the drive string and clamping string.

78

Figure 16.1: Taping strips enamel side own on table

Chapter 17
Glue Selection.   Mixing the Glue. Applying the Glue

What glue should I use? Much debate is tossed around about this subject as with anything else in making a fly rod. Resorcinol? It leaves purple lines at the joints. Some rod makers like that effect. Epoxy? Very strong but hard to work with, messy and extremely hard to sand or should I say file and sand. I use Urac 185 . This product is tried and true, although it has been taken out of production and now is replaced by Unibond, which is distributed by the same supplier. Both are strong and easy to use. It is economical and has a good working time and is easily mixed. The one small disadvantage is that it has a shelf life. The shelf life can be extended up to one year if kept refrigerated. It gets my vote as the glue to use. As I mentioned, Nelson Paint Company has now replaced Urac 185 with UniBond. I have used it and it works well. I use the mixing agent with the medium color.
I related a story at the beginning of my book about mixing glue. You remember the white lab coat crack, story at the beginning of my book about mixing glue. The guy gave me one as a

joke. I talked about mixing Urac 185 until it had the consistency of molasses. If you like numbers, 2 parts solid to 4 parts liquid it is too thick and 1 to 4 is too thin. Somewhere in between is just right.

This has worked great for me over the years. As far as the scale my friend bought, I was a little neurotic about mixing glue when I first got started and will now admit that I bought one. It does come in handy checking the weight of the various rods that you make. I used it once to see the difference in weight between my regular 8' 5 wt. and my 8' 5 wt. hollow built. Hollow builds are worth making when you make larger rods. It cuts the weight down by approximately 20%

Chapter 18
Gluing

I like to start gluing the butt section first. It is the easier section to glue. I would recommend that you do 2 or 3 dry runs without the glue applied to get used to the process, especially on the tips.

18.1 Gluing the Butt Section

I rigged up a system that holds my butcher paper, which allows it to reel off onto the table nearby the binder. Butcher paper works well for gluing. You get a great contrast from its white background. I apply the glue with the slick side of the paper facing up. The glued strips lift easily off from that side. After the rod section goes through the binder, I simply fold the paper over in half to use the rough side of the paper for rolling and wicking. If you don't want to invest in a roll of butcher paper, you can use freezer paper that is sold in small quantities.

Take your taped up strip and lay it on top of the paper. Use a razor blade to cut through the tape, making sure that the cut travels down between the same two strips being careful not to cut into the bamboo. Once the three pieces of tape have been cut, use your fingers to spread out the strips pressing them down to be flat on the table. Make sure that no debris is sitting on the strips by using a small paintbrush to clean the opened strips. Before you mix or apply the glue, make sure that your binder is ready to go by setting up the drive belt and threading the binding string through the tensioners. Use a large kitchen-measuring spoon to dip the liquid portion of the glue into a $1\frac{1}{2}$ oz. plastic mixing cup. Use another mixing cup to hold the hardening powder. Stir with a small wooden stick or a plastic mixing stick.

Apply the glue with a plumber's flux brush. Apply the mix liberally making sure all surfaces of the strips are covered. Lift the strips off from the table and press them back to the hex pattern using your fingers.

Figure 18.1: Gluing

Place the butt in the binder small end (ferrule end) first and attach the drive belt and string. Tie off the string using 3 half hitches and then start running your strip through the binder. Make sure that you stop to remove the tape as the butt travels along. When one direction is complete, again place the blank back into the binder, ferrule end first. This time reverse the wraps on the drive belt so that the string will go the opposite direction forming an crosshatch pattern on the blank. When binding is completed, place the blank back on the table after folding the paper in half and then use the palms of your hands to roll the blank as you would roll out dough. This ensures the strips are together and will help take out any bends. Doing this also wicks off excessive glue. Sight down the blank to look for bends, it should be almost perfectly straight. If not, tweak it a little. Hang the blank in a warm area of the house or in a drying cabinet from the ferrule end of the butt. Place a little string at the top and tie in a loop so it will fit on a cup hook. Place some more string at the bottom and tie on a 2lb. weight. Put something near the weighted end of rod so it won't spin.

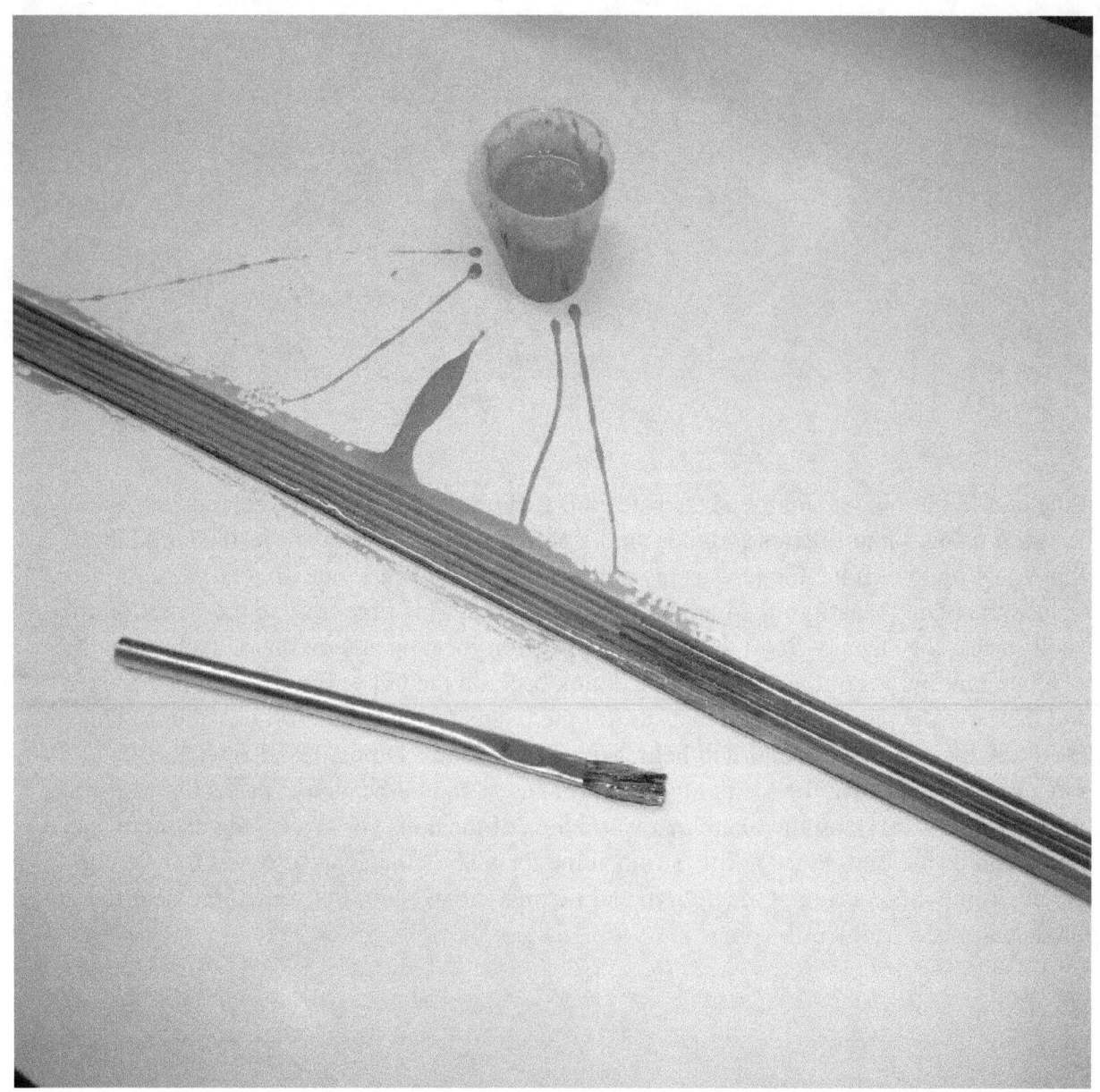

Figure 18.2: Glue application

18.2 Gluing the Tip Section

Follow the same procedure as you did with the butt. Since the tip is quite small, you may want to dry run this one to get used to how the last part of the tip will bend in the binder. The tip section goes through ferrule end first, narrow end follows through last. On the second pass increase the tension of the drive belt. I use my finger and thumb near the tensioner on the front of the binder to do this. If you use the Garrison binder with weights, increase the weight several ounces on the second pass. This compensates for some twisting that takes place on the first run through. When the tip is completed, place it into the butt side of the metal planing form. Tape it into the form with ¾" masking tape. Run your fingers up and down the length of the taped section using firm pressure. This helps to minimize bending of the tip that can occur, and cuts down on the amount of straightening to be done later. Let the blank dry overnight. The tip strip may be stuck in the form once it dries so remove it carefully with finger pressure starting at the ferrule end. Remember to clean off any glue that may build up on the form before you plane another set of strips. Goof Off works best for this.

Figure 18.3: Binding the glued strips

86

18.3 Removing String and Excess Glue

Your blanks have dried over night and it is time to sand off the string and make sure that all the dimensions are correct. I use an old board that I found in the basement of my friend's Victorian house. It is a 1" by 6" piece of fir that is about 5' long.

I place that board on top of my worktable. I work on the butt section first. Heck I forgot something. Remember the pencil marks you put on the strips? In case you can't see them all, enough of them will still be present to be seen on the glued blank. Take the butt over to your metal planing form. Align the butt to correspond with the marks on it. with the marks on the form. Darken each mark on one flat of the blank with your pencil or China marker. Use the sanding block and wrap it with 60 grit sandpaper. Now start at the grip end and sand off the string and excess glue. Do this all the way down the flat to the ferrule end. Make sure that you hold the block in such a way that you do not round off the edges on the blank.

We want well-defined edges that have not been rounded. Do not sand the string off the flat that you have marked. Once all flats have been sanded except the marked one, transfer the marks with the string still on them to a flat that has been sanded. Now sand off the string on that remaining flat. KEEP THOSE MARKS, THEY ARE IMPORTANT. The next step involves scrapping any remaining glue or string off the flats using a sharp razor blade. You will be using many razor blades building rods, so when they are on sale, buy several packs. They are usually sold in boxes of 100. Don't use dull blades to do your work. Blades are cheap, and once they become dull, dispose of them.

Start to use a razor blade to evenly scrape off the excess glue, and, or, the remaining string on one of the unmarked flats. Turn the blank 180° and do the same to that opposite flat. Do this until the marks still present on one flat are left. If you turn the blank 180° at some point and see the marks, carefully transfer them to an adjacent flat, as occasionally, you will accidentally scrape off a mark or two. You should have enough marks so you can put the strip back into your form aligning enough marks to replace the marks you scraped off.

You should now have a clean blank. The trouble is it may not show the proper final taper numbers at each mark (station) anymore. The glue tends to grow the dimensions and besides, the small errors you may have made will add up once the strips are glued together, yielding a fatter rod than the numbers should be. This error exists almost 100% of the time, which makes the rod over built.

Figure 18.4: Sanding off binding string

Now that we have the strips glued together to form a blank, keep in mind that the total diameter is now twice of what the planing form dimensions were. Place a sheet of paper near you while you are working the blank down to the final numbers. This piece of paper will have a notation of all the rod diameter numbers at all of the stations on the rod. This step confused me at first because it took me a long time to get the strips to conform to the target numbers that I wanted so I did not understand why I had to do this stuff now as I was so careful planing to 0.001". Well, it is just the way it is. Using razor blades, proceed scraping at each station on the blank blending to the next station on one flat. Rotate the blank 180° to the opposite flat and scrape off an equal amount, always checking the measurements until they are close to the target diameter numbers. Do this slowly and carefully until you get familiar with the process. After building many rods I find that I have made adjustments that lessen this process. These adjustments mostly consist of practice after making a few rods. In the meantime you will just have to grind it out and find out it is the way it is.

My first fly rod took me at least 120 hours to make, so don't get discouraged about the time you are spending on your first rod. This conclusion should make sense and it is obvious.

You will now start preparing your tip section. First cut the smallest end of the tip section with a Dremel tool with a diamond cut off wheel inserted in it. Cut the blank at the mark you made at that first station on the planing form, this way if you lose some of the marks on the tip section you can reference them back to first station number on the form. Before you begin to sand, you must check the tip sections for twists. We will treat the bends (straightening) and twists later on. If twists are present in the tip section, you will have a difficult time following the sanding block down the blank, especially as it becomes narrow. There would be a tendency to round off the corners of the blank, because the flat would tend to wander over. Set up your heat gun and turn it on low heat. Lay your section on a flat surface and carefully follow a flat down towards the tip top location. If the flat tends to drift over to another side, locate that point and bring it over to the heat gun. Heat the section up at that location, and with both hands and fingers apply twisting pressure in the opposite direction of the twist on the blank. Once you are satisfied that the twists have been removed, you can continue to sand off the string.

Sometimes I will use 150 grit sandpaper to sand off string on the tip section instead of using 60 grit. Remove the string and excess glue using the same method that you used on the butt section. Make sure that before you begin, you have clearly marked all of the stations on one of the flats by placing the tip blank back into the planning form.

After the string and excess glue has been sanded off, put your caliper on the first station of the sanded blank near the ferrule portion of the blank and take a reading. It will probably be a few thousandths of an inch over your target number. After you sand, use a new razor blade and work it up and down through the high station down to the next one as you did before.

You don't just want to reduce the size at the station only. You want to blend the dimensions from one station to the other. Flip the rod (180°) to the opposite flat and do the same thing. Check your measurements on all flats often as you work your way down the blank. After working your way down the rod, check all station measurements including the ones at the cut marks, to make sure that they are within 0.001" of your target numbers. If they are high, repeat the process. You want to be within 0.001" when you are finished. While you are doing this, you will sometimes move your marks to the next flat over. As you progress down the rod use even long strokes while taking off material, always blending into the next station. If you should have flats greater or lesser than your targets just average them out.

It is now time to cut the blank to size. Refer to chapter (19) and study the chapter on relating the butt to the tip before you cut anything. You should still have your cut marks on the blank. If you lost your cut marks, place the blank in the form and reference the marks you do have making new cut marks at the appropriate locations. You can cut the blank with a small handsaw with a fine blade or band saw if the blade is not too aggressive. Make the cuts a little more than half way through and then start sawing on the opposite side so that you don't get a tear out. I use a Dremel with an SS cutting wheel to cut the tip section at the tip top location. I then sand the flats with 220 or 320 grit paper using a block. Make sure not to round your edges. Use 0000 steel wool to finish up the flats.

Chapter 19

Relating the butt strips to the tip strips

When I was researching information on making bamboo fly rods, I never found any concise information describing how to relate the butt section to the tip section. The only information that I found said to the cut each section to be within 0.001" where they met. Before I describe my method, I will talk a bit about the dimensions where you join the butt to the tip. The most often used and easiest method is to make the cuts within 0.001" of each other where they meet. This will assure that the taper of the rod, is continuous. I found that through experimentation, you can make a jump at this point by having the butt cut be perhaps 0.005" or so greater than the tip section. This will normally speed up the action of the rod and I like that result on my rods.

You already have the tip at the correct length and that is easy to determine. Now how will you determine how the same length butt section will relate to the tip on the finished rod?

Your butt and tip section have been glued up with the string and the glue has been sanded and scraped to the taper numbers every 5 inches along their lengths, Now It is time to cut the sections to length and relate them to each other that so the taper is continuous when the rod is joined together.

This is fairly easy when you have a form that does not have the machined swelled butt groove like my Wagner. With a non-swelled butt form, or the Bellinger swelled butt form follow this procedure.

Place your tip section in the form with the narrowest taper grove on the right (tip top) and travel down the form towards the ferrule end. On a 7 foot six inch five weight rod, the last station on the tip before making the cut is .102 (on my taper sheet). Notice that I will also place the first station mark that will be on the butt on the tip side of the form. If you measure from the CUT MARK (on the tip station form) to station 107 you will find that it is 4 ¾ of an inch. Essentially the cut mark on the tip and the cut mark on the butt are the same, excluding the dam thickness inside of the female ferrule and also the wall thickness of the male ferrule. I consider this tiny amount to be unimportant.

Now, turn the form over to the butt side. Make sure that the grip end (widest taper grove) is on your right. Look down the form to the left and count up 4 stations (on most rod lengths that you make) At the dowel or station mark (depending on the brand of planing form you have) draw a line and label it .102 (for my 7 foot 6 inch five wt. rod). Use your dial gauge and set that station to .102. Now measure up 4 ¾ and you will draw another line which will read .107 (first station of the butt section). Remember that on the tip side of the form that the cut mark was 4 ¾ from the station .107. Another way to look at it would be the cut mark is ¼ inch to the left of the station 102 on the tip side of the form. On the butt side of the form, you will now place a Q-tip with one end cut off into the 13/64 female ferrule. Put the Q-tip exactly on the cut mark. Holding the Q-tip there, remove the ferrule leaving the Q-tip in place. Draw a line there, which will represent where the butt section is cut. Note that the end of the ferrule will be to the left of the cut mark. Draw a second line on the form there and label it rod end. If you were to hold the two sections together before ferruling them, the tip section would be longer than the butt section. The reason is, the female ferrule is longer than the male ferrule. Now you have a reference point, which is the rod end when the ferrule is lying on the form. From that place (rod end, not cut mark) measure up towards the grip 45 3/8 inches and draw a line, which will represent the end of the butt section once the reel seat is installed. This process will assure that the taper is continuous along the fly rod when it is put together.

Work out this drill a few times until it makes sense to you.

On the Wagner swelled butt form, plane the tip strips like you would on any other form. Once they are completed and glued together place the form with tip side up and the narrow taper (tip top end) on your right. Again, note the location of the cut mark. Fig 19.1

Figure 19.1: Where to cut tip picture below

You should have the first station of the butt also labeled on the tip. It will be 4 ¾ to the left on a 7' 6" rod. On the Wagner swelled butt form, plane the tip strips like you would on any other form. Once they are completed and glued together place the form with tip side up and the narrow taper (tip top end) on your right. Again, note the location of the cut mark. Fig 19.1 19.2. You should have the first station of the butt also labeled on the tip. It will be 4 ¾ to the left of the cut mark on a 7' 6" rod. Make a line at that point, which will represent the end of the rod at the butt location. Place the ferrule there and insert a Q-tip. Put a female ferrule on the Q-tip as you did before. Draw a line at the ferrule end. This will represent the rod end. Hold the Q-tip in place on the form and remove the ferrule. The end of the Q-tip will represent the butt cut mark. Draw a line there. From that line, measure to the right 4 ¾ inches and draw a line. This will be the first station on the butt section (107). Then measure up every 5 inches from that mark and draw lines. These lines will be your station locations on the butt. From the mark you made labeled rod end, measure up the form 45 3/8 inches. This will be the butt rod end.

Locate the beginning of the machined butt groove. Measure up above this location 3 inches and draw a line. This is where you will begin the cork grip. Decide how big of a grip you want. Measure up that distance and draw a line. This space will be occupied by.

19.2: Relating butt to tip (cut mark at male ferrule on tip will be at same location as cut on butt) Distance from that cut to station 107 on butt side of form is 4 3/4 inches.

the cork. measure up 3 1/2 inches and draw a line. This is the space the reel seat will occupy. I use 3 ½ for cap and bands as well as screw locking, and I use 3 5/8 for the mushroom seats that I use. The difference on the Wagner form is that the station marks will no longer correspond to the dowel pins and will make setting the form a bit more difficult

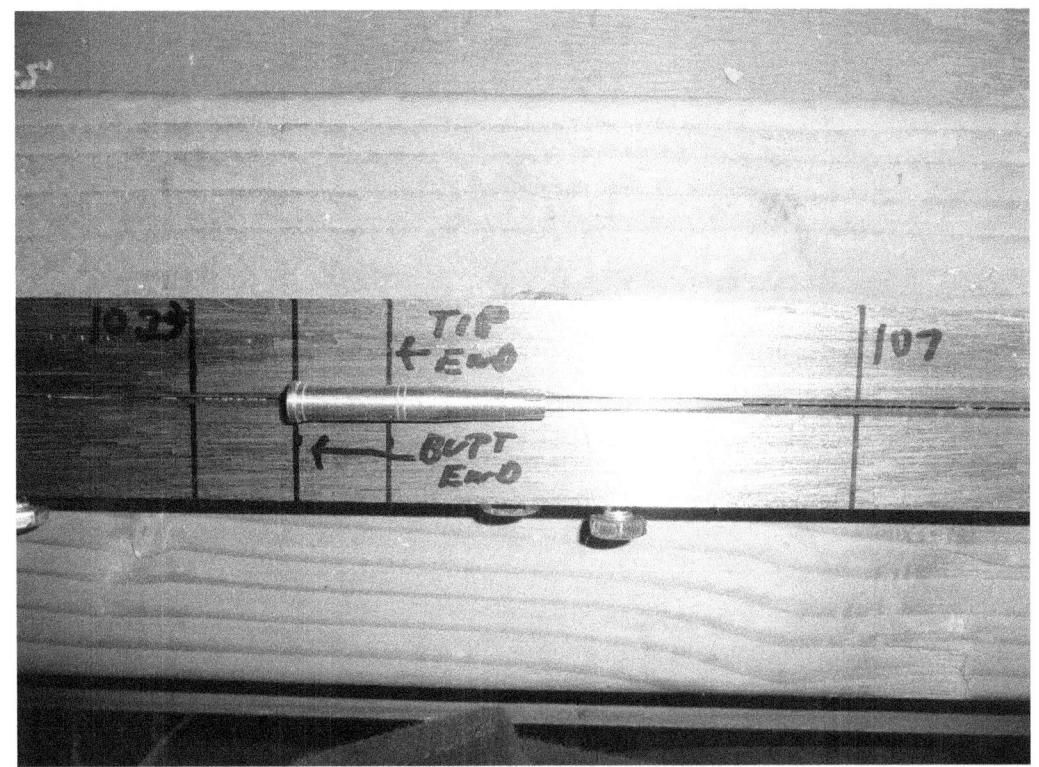

Fig.19.3 Toothpick shows where the butt will be cut. It is essentially at the same place the tip is cut

Chapter 20

Preparing the Ferrules

I use Super Swiss style ferrules made from nickel silver. You will find ferrules are fairly expensive when made from nickel silver. Do not use cheap, non-nickel ferrules. There are various suppliers from which to buy them. A few would be Classic Sporting Enterprises, J.D. Wagner Rod maker, (CSE) Bellinger (who distributes CSE ferrules and they put a small knurl on the female ferrule to match their reel seat hardware) Angler's Workshop, Rush River rods and Golden Witch. (See Appendix suppliers)

Ferrules are measured in 1/64ths (which equals .015) at their inside diameter. Common sizes for two piece bamboo fly rods are 13/64" and 12/64", sometimes 11/64" for small rods. The taper information that you will find will usually list the ferrule size to be used. If the ferrule size is unknown, use this formula. The way to determine what size ferrule is needed is to measure the diameter of the rod on opposing flats at the ferrule station and divide that measurement by .015" .For example, a 2 piece rod that measures 0.206 at the ferrule station would require a 13/64 ferrule 0.206 ÷ .015 = 13.7 or 13/64 ths). Taper information can be obtained at David Ray's Taper Library, and hexrod.net. Another useful provider of information would be High Sierra Rod Company. Once on their site, you can download the rod DNA program. It is available for PC as well as Mac. That program offers much useful information.

Ferrules are manufactured so that you have to prepare them to fit together. They are usually about 0.001" oversized. I will explain how to fit them once we glue them on the blank. Before they can be glued their slotted tabs must be crowned using sandpaper. I use 3M 400 and 220 grit wet/dry. I place a small square of 400 between two tabs and sand the edges of each tab until they are rounded and to a slight point. The 220 grit should now fit into the slots. This

coarser grit speeds up the process. I then reverse the direction using 220 grit and do the other sides of the tabs to match the first ones that were sanded.

Figure 20.1: Crowning ferrules

Once you have crowned both ferrules (Fig20.1) take some of the same paper and spin the end of the male ferrule (tab end) in the paper held between your fingers. It is a good idea to have this part of the ferrule tapered down a bit

The blank is now ready to go into the lathe and be prepared to accept the ferrules

20.1 Marking the Blank before Fitting the Ferrule

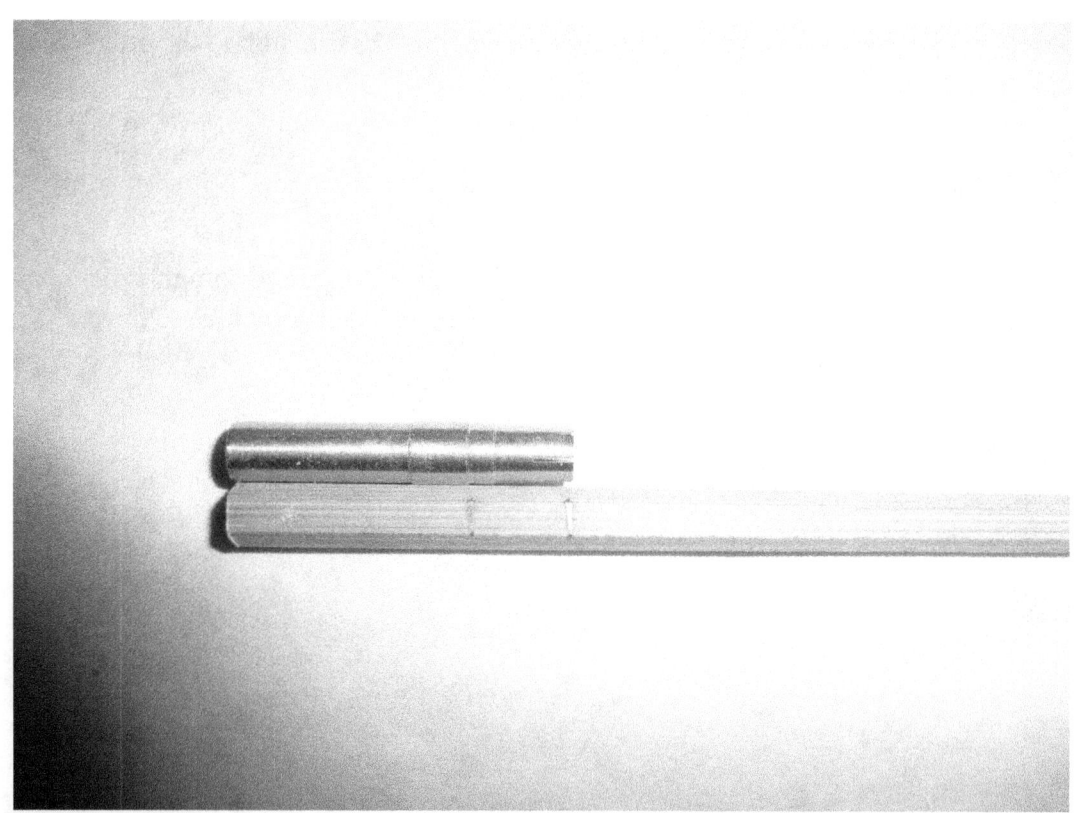

Figure 20.2: Above-Marks on blank for ferrule

Transfer the ferrule marks to both the butt and tip blanks. Fig. 20.2. Place the blank in the lathe so that the second mark extends slightly beyond the chuck jaw. Fig 20.5. Make sure that your lathe is equipped with a 3-jaw chuck. I use masking tape wrapped around the blank as it enters the lathe to protect the blank. You will have to support the portion of the rod where it extends opposite of the lathe chuck jaws. I sometimes use some ¼" pine uprights with holes drilled through them to achieve this. I now use uprights used for wrapping the rod. Fig. 21.7. Use one upright for the butt, and two for the tip. I then secure the lathe chuck jaws making sure that you get a true spin. Do not have the lathe set at too high of a speed as you will not use lathe cutting tools to round you blank. Instead, you will be using a small piece of wood and a piece of 60-grit sandpaper. Some rod makers change to 150 grit before getting a close fit. (I have seen one maker use a commercial grade woman's emery fingernail file to do this operation). Be careful not to take off too much material. Start at the cut end and hold the block and small piece of paper up to its edge and begin taking off material until it becomes round. Periodically stop the lathe to see if you are getting close to a snug fit

Place the ferrule on the blank and try to slip it on. When you start to get a fit rotate the ferrule several times onto the blank. When it will not continue any further up the blank, take it off. You will notice that a black mark from the ferrule will be left on the blank, (Fig. 20.5) this indicates the high area where more material must be removed. Continue this process until the end of the tabs reach the mark closest to the lathe jaws. Do not round the blank past the one closest to the chuck. This operation should be done slowly and carefully. The ferrule should have a tight fit when you are done. Do not take off too much material or this will result in a loose fit. If the ferrule sticks on the blank during this process do not try to remove it with pliers, as you will damage the ferrule. I use a small piece of 600 grit wet/dry between my fingers to twist the ferrule off. You might have to really bare down on it to remove it. Fig. 20.4.

Figure 20.4: Removing stuck ferrule

There is nothing more irritating than having one of the ferrule pieces slip off from the rod while casting or when breaking down the rod. When I began making rods I was using the recommended slow set epoxy to glue on ferrules. Even though I had a tight fit between the blank and the ferrule, I still had some ferrule failures. I decided to change glue. I now use an expansion type product. Gorilla glue works fine for this.

Clean the inside of both ferrules using a Q-tip that has been dipped in denatured alcohol. Before you apply the glue, wet the end of the blank where the ferrule will be placed and apply a liberal amount of glue. I use a bamboo shish kabob stick to apply glue during this step and use a similar stick when I epoxy on reel seats. Push the ferrule on the blank and make sure that it goes on all the way such that there is no air pocket. The ferrule should end up with the serrations in the ferrule centered on a flat. The serrations don't go even with the hex edges Wipe off the excess glue with a wet paper towel and make sure that the

Figure 20.5: Marks on blank picture

with the hex edges Wipe off the excess glue with a wet paper towel and make sure that the glue is cleaned off the flats near the ferrule.

With the blank parallel to the ground, bang the end of the ferrule against a hard surface. Don't let your wife see you doing this on the edge of her kitchen counter. Take the ferruled blank over to a bench and tightly wind nylon string or cord around the ferrule. Make sure the cord goes around the ferrule tabs. Fig. 20.6. Set aside to dry. Do not attempt to fit the ferrules until they dry for at least 12 hours.

20.2 Gluing the Ferrule

There is nothing more irritating than having one of the ferrule pieces slip off from the rod while casting or when breaking down the rod. When I began making rods I was using the recommended slow set epoxy to glue on ferrules. Even though I had a tight fit between the blank and the ferrule, I still had some ferrule failures. I decided to change glue. I now use an expansion type product. Gorilla glue works fine for this.

Clean the inside of both ferrules using a Q-tip that has been dipped in denatured alcohol. Before you apply the glue, wet the end of the blank where the ferrule will be placed and apply a liberal amount of glue. I use a bamboo shish kabob stick to apply glue during this step and use a similar stick when I epoxy on reel seats. Push the ferrule on the blank and make sure that it goes on all the way such that there is no air pocket. The ferrule should end up with the serrations in the ferrule centered on a flat. The serrations don't go even with the hex edges Wipe off the excess glue with a wet paper towel and make sure that the glue is cleaned off the flats near the ferrule. With the blank parallel to the ground, bang the end of the ferrule against a hard surface. Don't let your wife see you doing this on the edge of her kitchen counter. Take the ferruled blank over to a bench and tightly wind nylon string or cord around the ferrule. Make sure the cord goes around the ferrule tabs. Fig. 20.6. Set aside to dry. Do not attempt to fit the ferrules until they dry for at least 12 hours.

20.3 Bluing ferrules

If you would like to blue your ferrules or other hardware such as reel seat hardware, there are a variety of products sold for bluing guns. I have had excellent results using Van's Instant Gun Blue. I blue my ferrules after they are mounted on the rod. The surface should be roughed up using 600 or 1000 grit paper prior to bluing.

I have found that rubbing the bluing solution on with a dab of 0000 steel wool seems to work best. I then apply more solution with a Q-tip, rubbing briskly. After I get the desired color, I let the piece dry and then wipe with a soft cloth. It is best to coat the finished piece with lacquer. I like Staybrite or Mohawk clear gloss brass lacquer because it is durable and

protects against UV. I Mask off the male to prevent treatment where it enters the female. Plug the female ferrule to prevent solution from entering it. Fig. 20.7.

I then apply more solution with a Q-tip, rubbing briskly. After I get the desired color, I let the piece dry and then wipe with a soft cloth. It is best to coat the finished piece with lacquer. I like Staybrite or Mohawk clear gloss brass lacquer because it is durable and

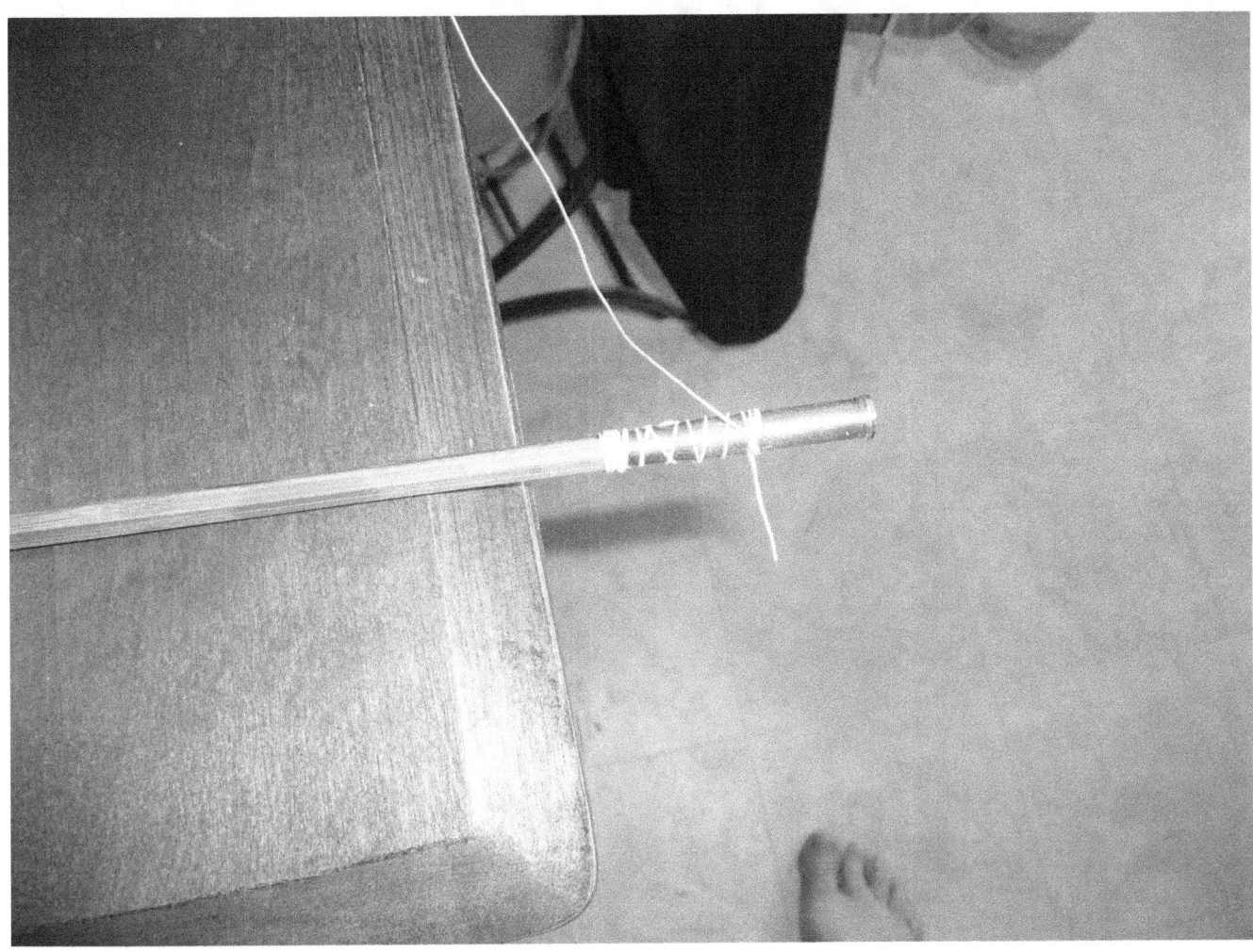

Figure 20.6: Wrapping the ferrule binds down the tabs until dry

Fig. 20.7. Masked off and plugged ferrules

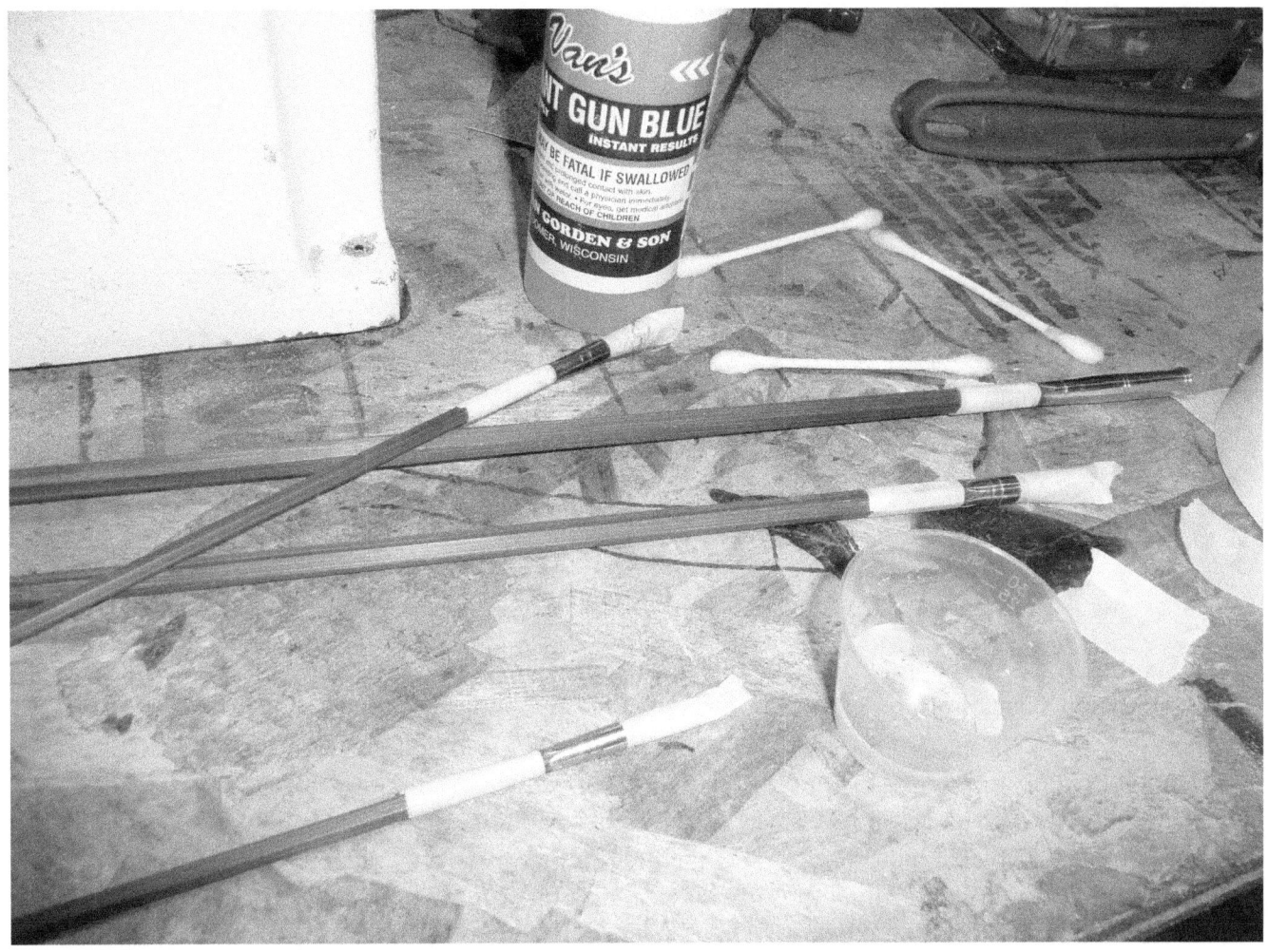

Fig. 20.8. Blueing ferrules

Chapter 21
Cork

Most bamboo rod makers prefer to make their own cork grips. It is fairly easy and provides satisfaction and a custom fit to your hand. There are various sources for cork that you can find on the Internet. I get mine from C and D Trading Company. It is available in various sizes and is graded for quality. I order E1R flor plus reserve. It can come in standard color or burl patterns, either light or dark. The dark burl is sometimes called burnt burl.

You will notice, as you use your fly rod, the handle becomes dirty and collects grime. Since I fish a lot, and my cork grips sometimes get disgustingly dirty, I occasionally clean them using Soft Scrub with bleach and a Scotch Brite pad. Unless you hang the rod on the wall the cork is going to get dirty. It is for this reason that I do not use the most expensive grade of cork. I buy rings that are 1¼" in diameter, ½" thick and have ¼" holes drilled through their center.

I am a traditionalist when it comes to hardware, silk wrapping and cork grips. I like a simple look to my rods. I think, elegance is best expressed by simplicity on bamboo fly rods. I am not one for fancy cork designs, engraved hardware, elaborate wrap colors and design, screw locking real seats, heavy coats of varnish and so on. This is your choice since it is your rod. The length of your grip depends on what you like, not just tradition. If you have a large hand you may want more than a 5½" grip as was used on most Leonard rods. I generally put on a 6" grip on smaller rods and a 6½" on 7½' and 8' rods. The number of cork rings required would be 11, 12 or 13 respectively. I mostly use what I call a modified cigar grip on my rods. Fig. 21.1. Full wells grips are also very nice. Fig. 21.2

Figure 21.1: Modified cigar

Figure 21.2: Full wells being shaped

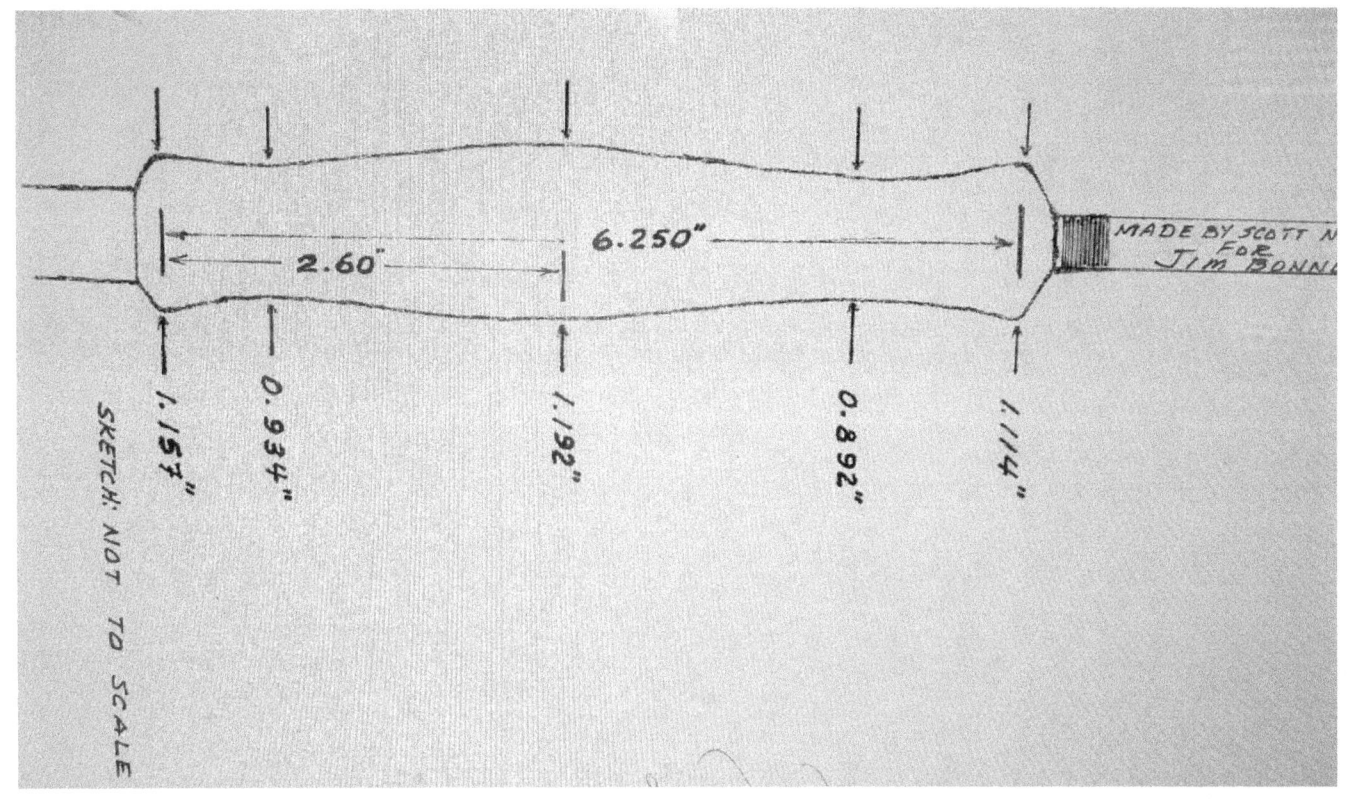

Figure 21.3: Full wells dimensional drawing

21.3 Make or buy a cork press?

Once your butt section's ferrule has dried for an hour or two you can glue on your cork rings with Tite Bond II or III. Before you start, you must ream out the holes in the center of the cork so that they will fit onto the blank. Buy a small size cork reamer. A cork reamer is a short piece of rod blank with abrasive particles glued to its surface. You can manually ream the cork or put the reamer in your lathe chuck jaws. Use a slow speed when reaming the cork with the reamer on the lathe. Work the cork up the reamer towards the chuck. You want to have a snug fit when the rings are slid down the blank from the ferrule end to the grip location. The cork that will be on the front portion of the rod should be reamed with a little smaller diameter hole than the other rings. You want the first cork ring to have a snug fit where it meets the bamboo. Label it first cork (FC) and put it on last.

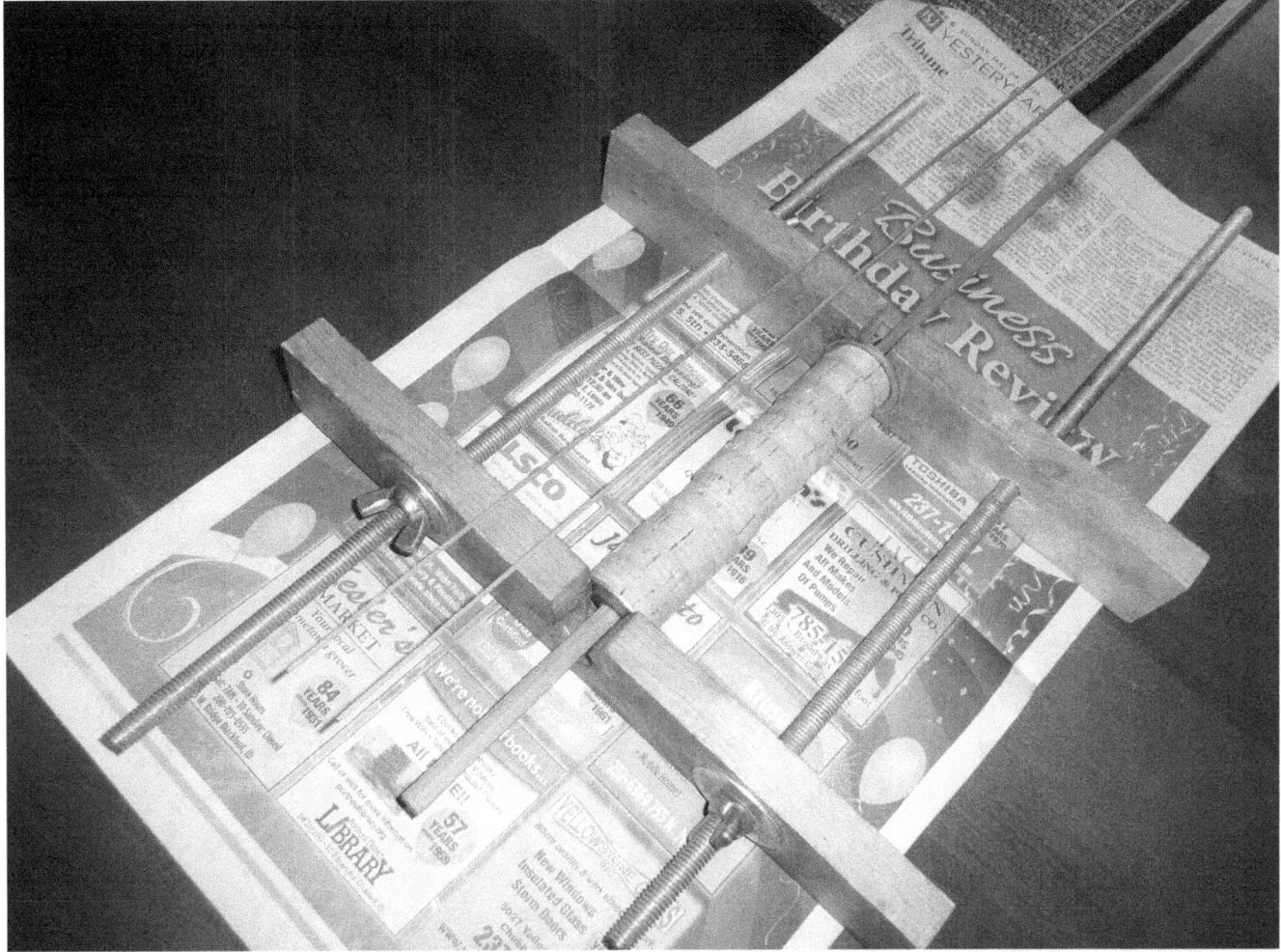

Figure 21.4: Homemade cork press

Figure 21.5: Above-Reaming the cork rings

The following procedure will apply when you are using a cap and band style reel seat.

Lay the rod down on a table and measure 3½" from its handle end (largest diameter of the rod). Draw a line there. Measure down the rod the distance that your cork will occupy. If you half a 6½" grip (13 cork rings) measure down 6½" and draw another line. These lines will reference the positioning of the cork rings when you glue them on. Note that the reel seat space should be 3½" beyond the first cork placed on the blank. Before putting on the rings, file the corners of the bamboo down to accept a 3/8" inside diameter reel seat insert. This filing should go down from the butt end a little over 3½" so that when you mount the seat it will butt up snugly to the cork. Did you remember to cut the butt end to

the right length? Is the tip section the same length as the butt section?

Over a sink with water and a sponge handy, slide on the first cork down to the mark you made near the reel seat end. Its trailing edge will be on the line. Apply glue to the front of that cork holding the rod vertically. Apply glue all of the way around the face of that first cork. Slide the next cork down the rod to be next to the first cork. Rotate the second cork and push it hard against the first cork. Glue will be pressed out. Make sure that the first cork does not go behind the line that was placed near the location of the reel seat. Use your index finger to wipe the excess glue and apply it to the front of the next cork. Apply some more glue making sure that it covers around the cork's front surface, and slide on the next cork ring. Continue this process until all of the rings are in place. Wipe the excess glue off all rings with a sponge, so that no build up is left on, or around the flats. Now place the

cork into a press. Make sure that the rings are centered on the blank, especially at the back end where the reel seat hardware and wood insert will fit on. Tighten the press until you see some glue squeeze out, and form a slight bulge between the rings. The rings must be tight with no gaps showing. If you should decide to use an up-locking reel seat, the first cork put on must be prepared to accept the reel seat receiver. I use the proper size reamer bit placed in my drill press to accomplish this.

114

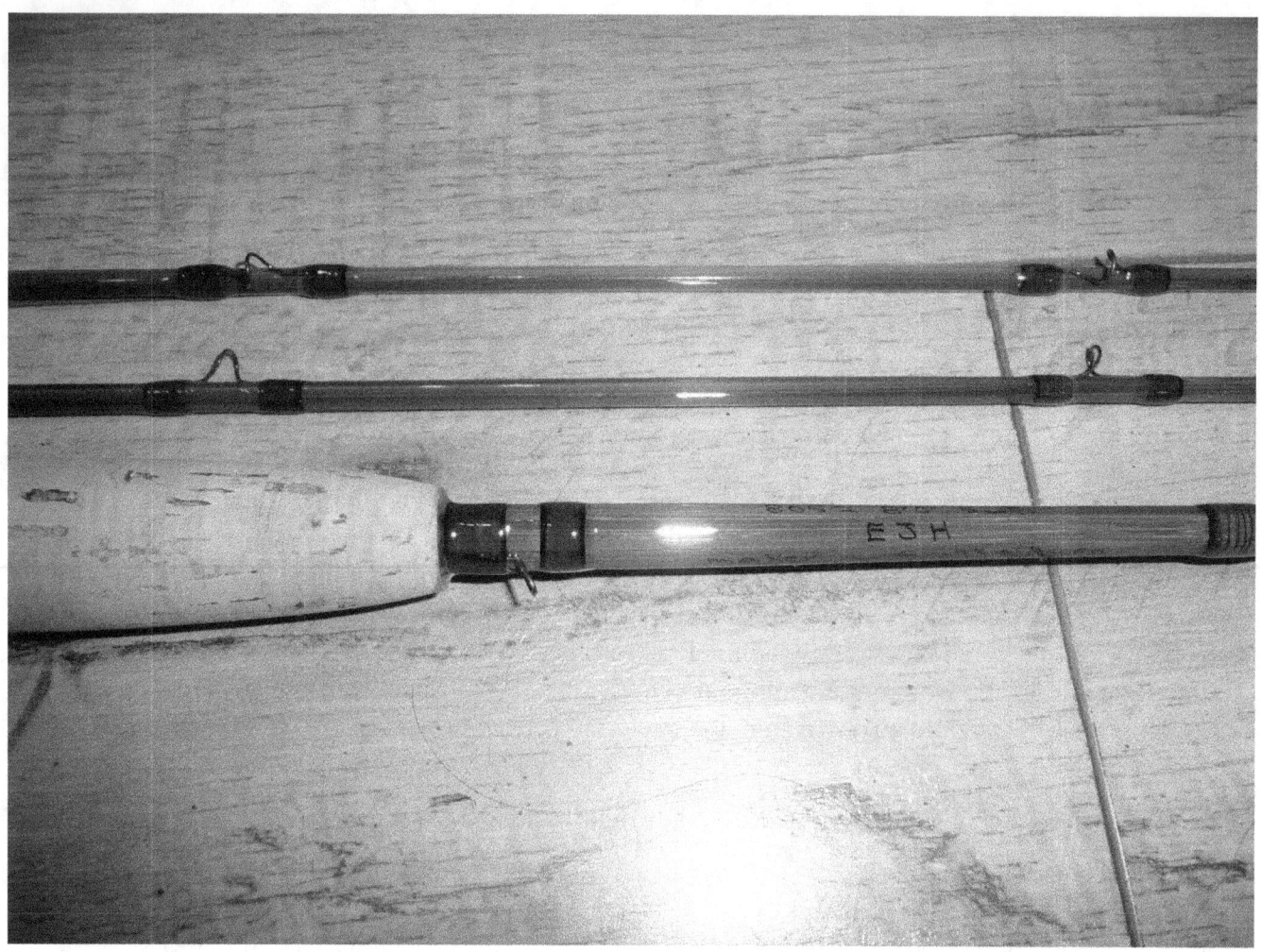

Figure 21.6: Leaving an edge on front of cork for using a thread winding check

21.2 Forming the Cork on a Lathe

After the glued cork rings have dried over night, remove the blank from the cork press. Sometimes you must use a razor blade to remove the cork from the press where it may have stuck to the wood on the press.

Use a large fender washer on each side of the cork before it is placed in the press, and apply vegetable oil to the washers, which prevents the cork from sticking.

Onward to shaping the cork handle.

Secure the reel seat end of your blank into the lathe chuck jaws. Make sure that the other end of the rod is supported. Fig. 21.7. Also make sure you are getting a true spin on the section with no wobbling. First, shape the cork using 60, 150, and 220 grit sandpaper. Arrive at your desired thickness and grip style chosen. Reduce the sandpaper grits and finish the cork handle by using 600 grit wet/dry sandpaper.

Figure 21.8: Shaping cork on the lathe

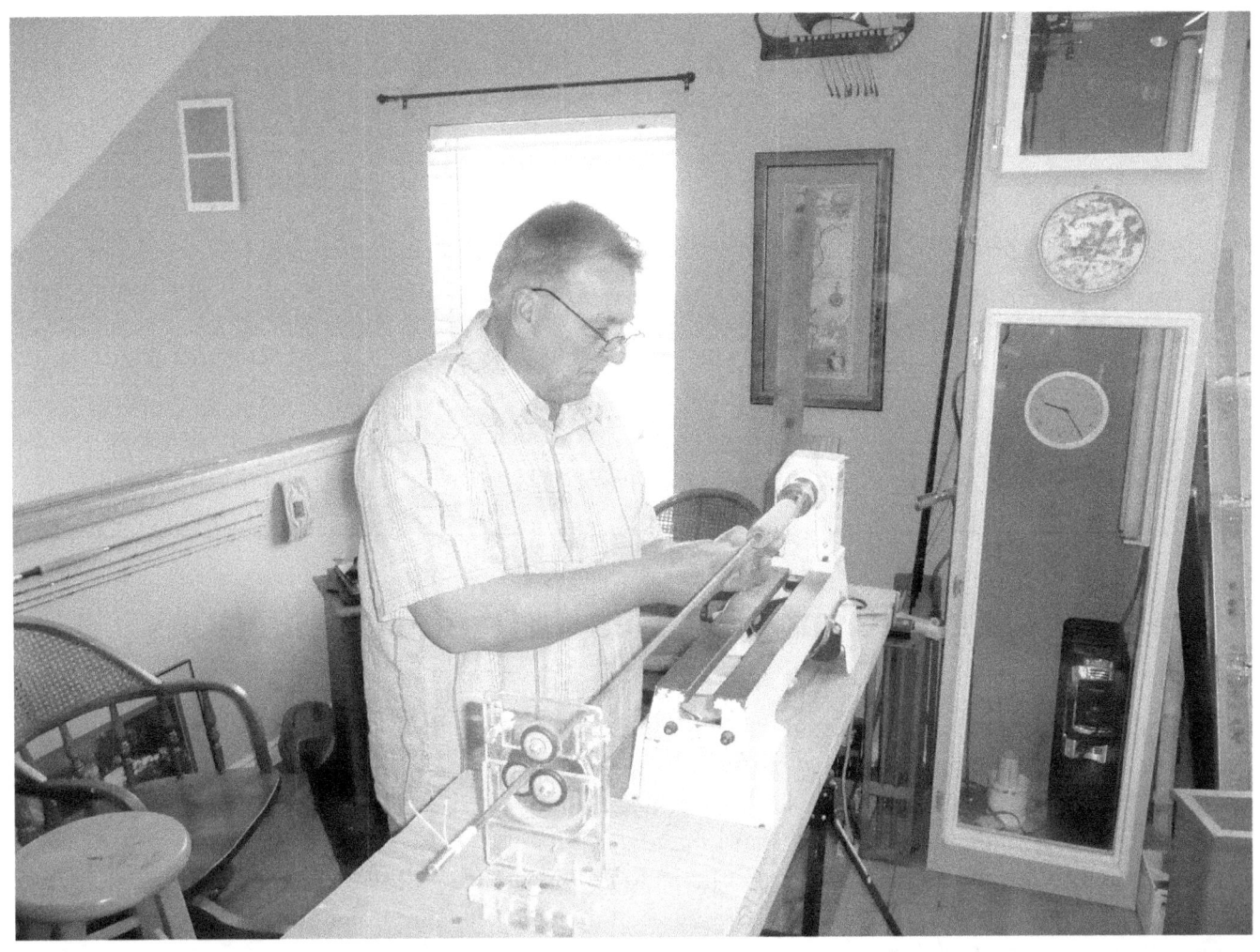

Figure 21.7: A support when a rod section is in the lathe

Chapter 22

Straightening... Removing Bends from the Sections

During the time I have been a rod maker, I have had little trouble with twists or sets with butt sections. Perhaps I am lucky or I just have done things right. If you should have problems with the butt, it will take longer to resolve them than it does to correct bends in the tip section. I have to straighten many tips that I make.

Lets see if your butt needs straightening. It helps to do this sighting down it against a white wall or building. If you see a bend, keep a finger on that spot during your sighting. Bends most often occur at a nodal area.

Straightening is done using the heat gun.

Have your heat gun mounted vertically so both of your hands are free to rotate the section while heating. If the gun has a temperature adjustment you should select the low or medium setting. Heat the area where the bend is located with one hand on either side and away from that area. Rotate the rod while heating. Note the orientation of which way the bend occurred, and heat around that area a full 360°. You can hold the rod fairly close but not right next to the gun. How much time is needed? It is better to start off with short periods of heating and work up to longer periods once you are accustomed to working with bends. Remember how fast the nodes scorched when you heated them during the node treatment step? Be careful, as a heat gun can produce temperatures upwards of 500°F.

Many of the steps in the rod building process require getting a feeling for. With practice you will become more proficient, but be aware, some of the steps can be subjective rather than objective. Bamboo rod making is not an exact science, which adds to the mystique and makes it kind of interesting.

You usually will not take out a bend during your first attempt. When I encounter a stubborn bend, I will attempt to correct it no more than three or 4 times and then set it aside for a while and continue later. This is especially true with the butt section. The thicker the bamboo the harder it is. Remember that the steps required to complete your rod demand patience and attention to detail.

I have a friend who neglected to check the butt section of his rod for straightness before heat-treating. He did not notice that there was a bad bend up near the grip. Unfortunately it was only noticed after he shaped the cork on the lathe. The finished grip looked like the hunch back of Notre Dame because of that bend. It should have been noticed and corrected earlier in the process. He asked me if his butt section could be rescued. This would be tough because of the thickness of the rod in the area. At this point all of the cork that was put on his rod had to be removed to correct the problem. I told him it would have been impossible to heat the rod up and try to use your hand and arm strength to take the bend out. The only chance was to soak that portion of the rod in water overnight and then heat it up and put it in a vise and really pull on it. After several attempts, he finally corrected the problem and learned a good lesson. Taking out bends in butt sections can be difficult and time consuming. Hopefully, if you have a bend in the butt, so to speak, it will be down stream of the grip and closer to the ferrule.

You will do the same thing with the tips except that they should not be heated as long. You will probably have at least 3 places to correct on a tip section, and remember that they will usually be at the nodes. Get the tip as straight as you can. Tiny bends are acceptable as far as performance is concerned, but should you decide to sell rods, any bend is bad news.

Chapter 23

Twists

Twists normally only occur in the tip sections. They are caused during the binding process while gluing up that section. The tip is run through the binder the first time with tension. This tension will tend to add some twisting action, especially down at the end near the narrow portion of the tip. I try to compensate for this by adding a little more tension to the drive belt when I make my second pass. My binder allows me to tighten the tension knob or also use my fingers on the continuous drive belt to add more pressure or tension. If you use a drive belt with a weight at the bottom you will have to add a little more weight during the second pass.

Twists in tips are easy to see. When tip sections are placed on a flat table one flat will begin to wander off to one side or another. The section of the rod also will tend to bounce or spring up when pressed down upon. If you have a twist, heat the area with your heat gun and then apply twisting pressure in the opposite direction of the twist that exists on the section. Again don't over heat, and do this slowly using more than one attempt if necessary.

Chapter 24

Preparing Ferrules to Accept the Thread

Figure 24.1: Removing bumps off ferrule tab

Use a razor blade to remove the string or cord that you wrapped tightly around the ferrule when you glued it on. The excess glue on it is easily removed using a new razor blade. Use caution not to nick or cut into the bamboo when you do this.

Place the butt section on a table or bench so you are looking down on the ferrule. Good lighting and perhaps a magnifier like the ones for fly tying will help you immensely at this point. Use your finger to feel the tab area where it meets the bamboo flats. You will notice there is a bump at this transition point. This must be worked smooth so the thread will climb up the ferrule when you wrap the rod. A diamond impregnated jewelers file works well for this. Place a ¾ inch piece of pine under the ferrule area to keep the rod elevated off from the table and carefully file down the tab edges. B careful not to knick the bamboo. Fig. 24.1. Rotate the rod until you get all of the high spots removed from the tabs. Check for any bumps or high spots that remain and smooth those off. Now use some 220 grit wet/dry paper to dress out the file marks. Reduce to 400, 600 and then 1000 grit, finishing off with 0000 steel wool. Do the same process with the tip ferrule.

24.1 Preparing the Male Ferrule for a Proper Fit

I mentioned that when you buy ferrules they are about 0.001" over sized. They will not join until they are prepared. The rod maker will want to prepare the ferrule so that he can achieve a fit that is to his liking. The goal is to end up with a smooth popping sound when the rod is broken down.

First clean the female ferrule by wrapping a small amount of 0000 steel wool on a bamboo shish kabob stick, and insert it into the female ferrule while rubbing vigorously back and forth inside the ferrule. After finishing the female, move on to the male. Cut a small square of wet/dry 400 about ⅜ × 3". I never really measure them. An auto paint supply shop is the best source to get your wet/dry paper. They have a selection in a variety of grits. I use a lot of 400, 600 and 1000. Also lots of 0000 steel wool. The other grades of regular sandpaper you will want are 60, 150, 220, and 350. These grits are usually found at any hardware store.

Chapter 25

Fitting The Ferrule

Take a small piece of 400 grit wet/dry between your fingers and start rotating the rod in your other hand. Do this so that you are taking equal amounts of material off the male ferrule along its length. Don't take off too much material in the beginning. Repeat this process with 600, 1,000, and 0000 steel wool. Fig. 25.2. After the steel wool, apply some dry Ivory bar soap to the male and see if you are starting to get a fit into the female ferrule. You must carefully repeat this process a few times. On subsequent trials, eliminate the 400 grit wet/dry. It will tend to take off too much material. I like a tight fit on my ferrules. I usually leave the ferrule a little on the tight side until after the rod is wrapped. I adjust it to a perfect fit before I use or ship the rod. When the male ferrule is properly dressed, the ferrule should make a pleasant popping sound when the rod is broken down. I like a tight fit on my ferrules. I usually leave the ferrule a little on the tight side until after the rod is wrapped. I adjust it to a perfect fit before I use or ship the rod. When the male ferrule is properly dressed, the ferrule should make a pleasant popping sound when the rod is broken down.

Fig.25.1:Removing burrs from the female

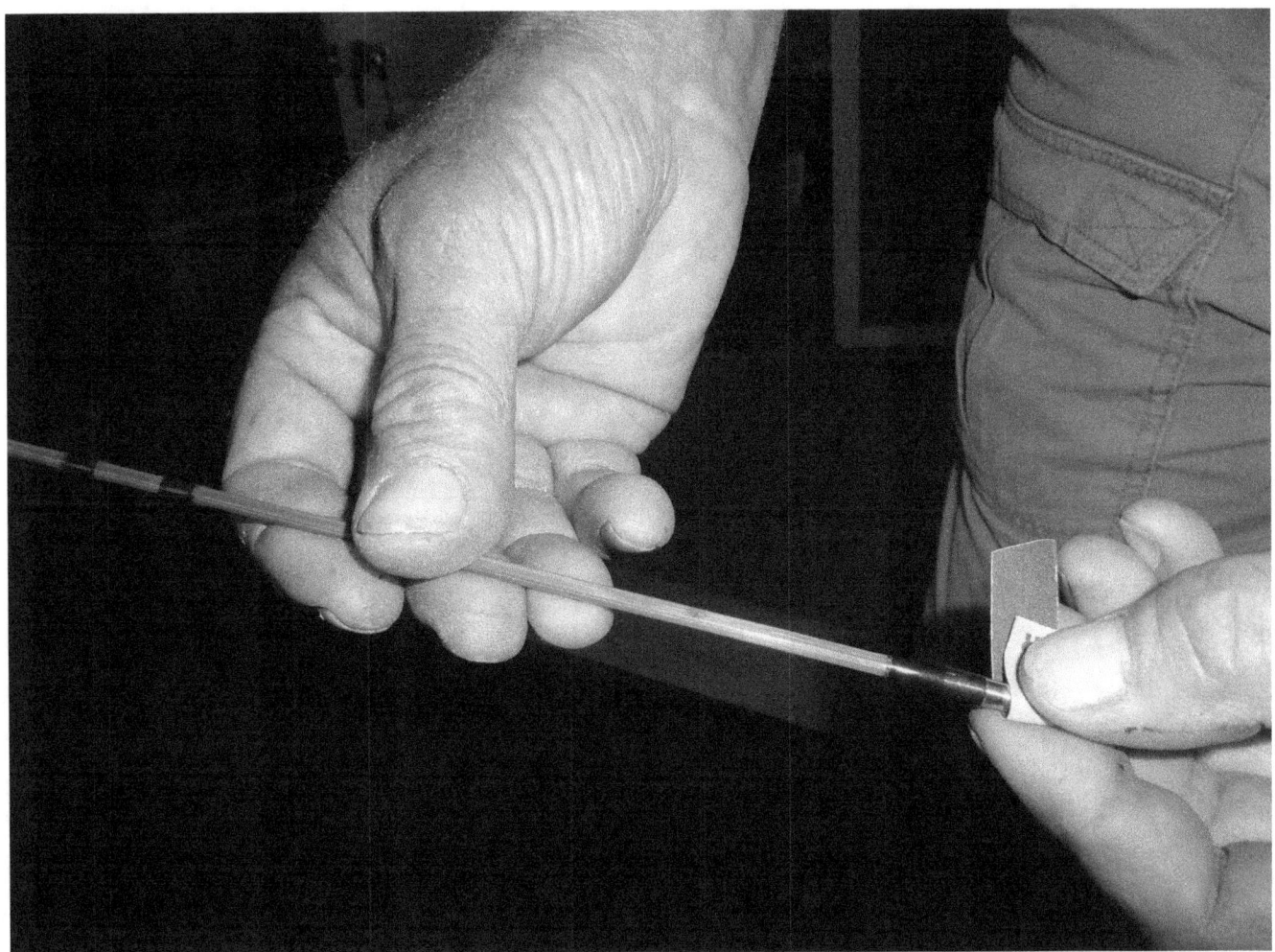

Figure 25.2: Sanding the male ferrule

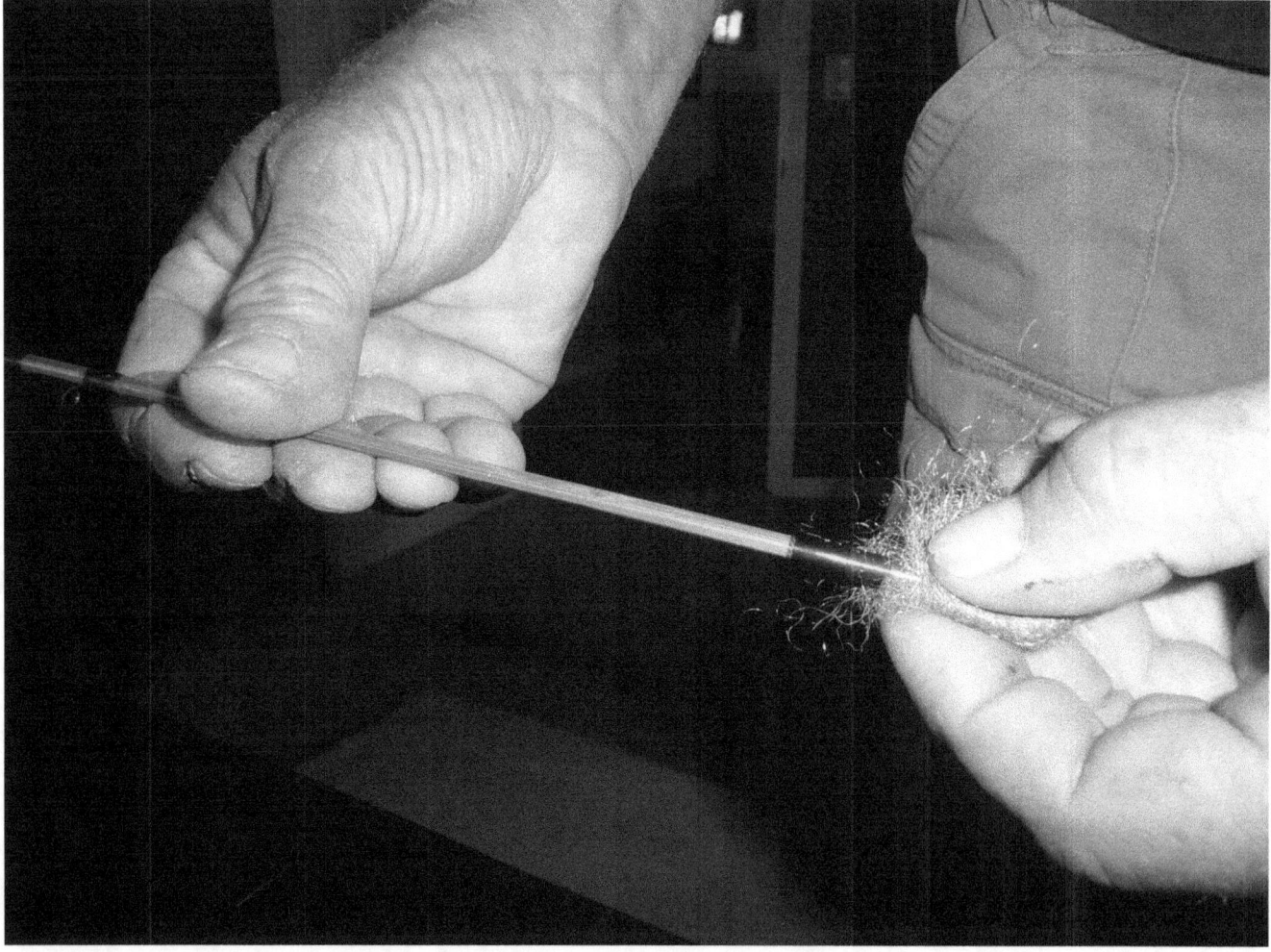

Figure 25.3: Using 0000 steel wool to fit the male ferrule

Chapter 26

Guide and Tip Top Locations

Unlike graphite rods, bamboo rods do not have a true spline. How you do determine on which flat to place the guides and what about the spacing of the guides? How many guides and what size? Usually when you look up a taper in order to build a rod, the taper information will indicate the ferrule size, the tip top size, the number of guides and the distances at which the guides are spaced. If you are building a rod other than the ones that I have proposed in this book, there are a number of sites on the Internet that will give you that information. In my family of rods I use one 10 mm agate-stripping guide and then #2 snake guides on the butt section. On the tip, I use six #1 snake guides. My tip tops are either size 4, or 5 depending on the rod size.

I determine the flat that the guides are to be placed on by putting the rod together and sighting down the rod to spot the natural drop of the rod. Because it is impossible to get the ferrule 100% true to center, there will always be a place where the rod will tend to droop down. You can then call the flat on top of the droop to be the spline and the bottom facing down to be the location of the guides.. I should mention that there are other techniques to determine the best way to identify the best flat to put the guides on. I have used lots of techniques. If you want to try alternative methods, here are a few of them.

1. You can use a spline finder and find where there usually is a tendency to find a stiffer side of the rod.
2. You can do the same thing without using the finder, but using your fingers to press on the center of the rod while it is held on the floor or a counter top. This works also, but can drive you crazy.
3. You can clamp a rod section to a table and pull down on the opposite end of the clamp. You then find the flat that has the best vertical up and down movement while looking opposite the clamp, rather than it having a circular motion. After one of these methods are used you can assemble the rod with your results marked on the rod and then give it a firm casting stroke and listen to the sound that it makes. You should notice that there will be one position that has the

highest pitched tone or sound. If you have had a musical background, this technique might interest you. The number 3 method often will indicate the best combination of two flats to accept the guides. To determine which one of those flats to use, assemble the rod to find the natural bend in the rod. Place the guides on the flat that droops down.

Before marking the guide locations, make sure that the rod has been straightened to your satisfaction and then install the tip top. You will be cutting some of the material off from the tip section in order to determine the tip top location. Place the tip section back into your planing form. The ferrule end will be lined up right at the cut mark on the form. Down at the other end put the tip top that you are using down at the end   so that the loop is right at the line representing the first or smallest station. Using a razor blade, prepare a toothpick so that it will seat into the tiptop. Fig. 26.1 With the toothpick seated in the tip top, and making sure that the ferrule is lined up with the cut line, remove the tip top and mark the bamboo so that it lines up with the end of the toothpick. Cut the excess off using a SS wheel on your Dremel tool.

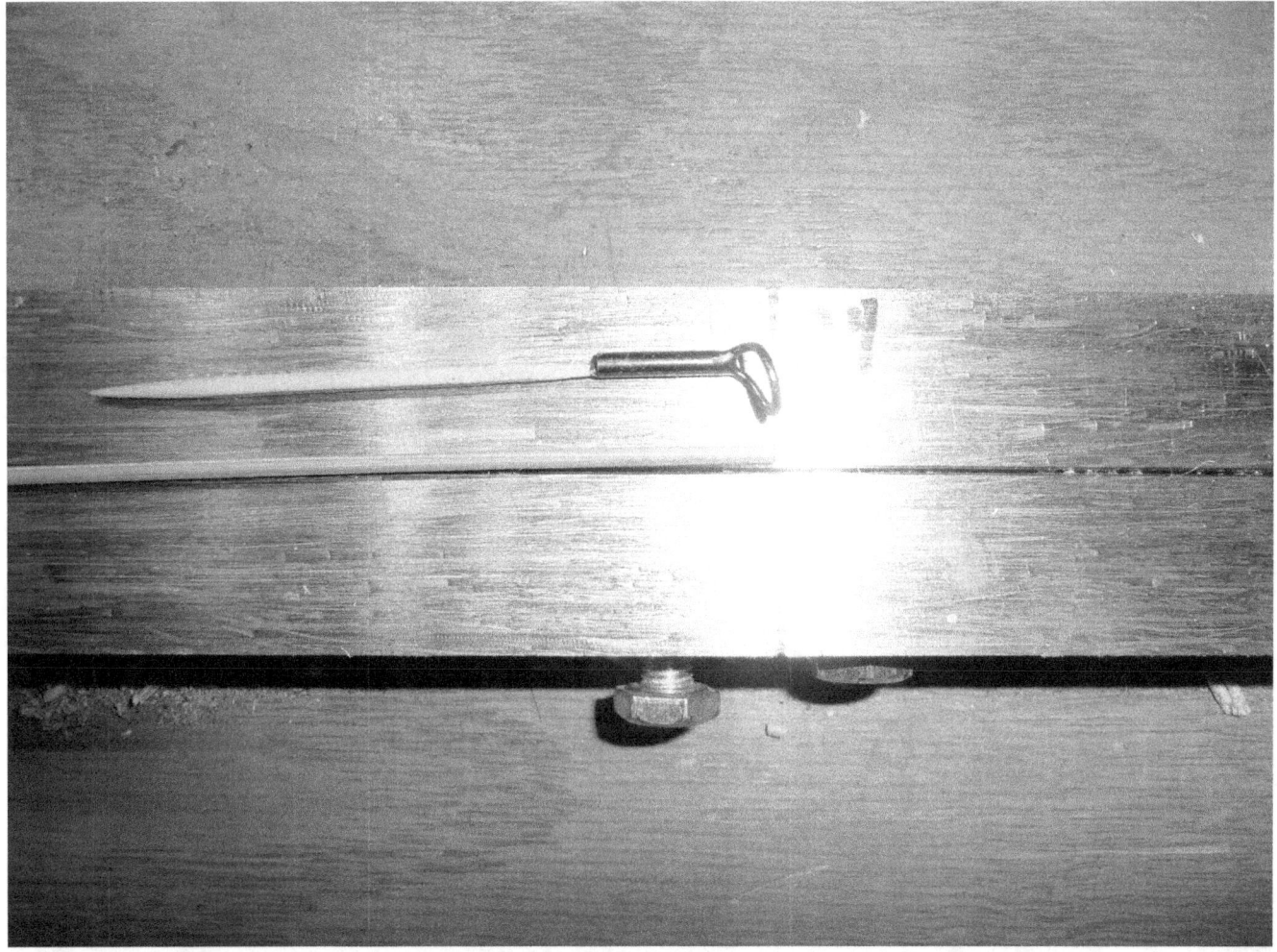

26.1: Above -Determining the tip top depth

Install the tip top using 5-minute epoxy. (I have never had a tiptop failure using 5 minute epoxy glue). Make sure that the tip top lines up pointing down opposite the flat that you have identified to be the spline. When it is dry, fit the rod together and place it on a bench or flat table.

You should have earlier marked the butt section where the reel seat will go with a mark that identifies its spline side. With the spline side facing up on the table rotate the rod 180°, and with a tape measure, put the zero inch mark right at the tip top and start measuring up the rod towards the cork. Guide measurements start at the tip and continue up the rod towards the cork grip. Mark each location with a white China marker. You are now ready to wrap.

Fig. 26.2: Cutting tip section to allow for tip top space it occupies

Chapter 27
Wrapping Your Rod

By the time I started making bamboo fly rods, I had already had some experience wrapping graphite rods. If you have never wrapped a rod before, you can rent or buy a video, or get information on the Internet. Like any other skill, you will improve with some practice. Fortunately for us, the wraps on bamboo rods are fairly simple when compared to the fancy patterns you often see on graphite rods. I have a friend who owns a terrific fly shop featuring rod-building supplies and he is probably the best wrapper I have ever seen. I would marvel at his work knowing that I probably could never attain his level of skill as he had wrapped at least 5,000 rods at this point. He offered me some good hints, but I didn't think it was necessary to take a class from him, since I would be making the simpler wraps often practiced on bamboo rods. I also found, wrapping bamboo rods was easier than wrapping graphite rods because the angles on a hex rod offer more resistance that holds the thread better than it is held on the slick and round surface of a graphite rod. Silk is a more difficult to wrap than nylon because it usually is quite a bit thinner and also it has some other different characteristics.

You will need to build or buy some sort of rod wrapper. I have one fancy, commercial wrapper, and I also have a wrapper I made using an old sewing machine motor. You do not have to have a power wrapper to get good results. You need to have a means of holding the rod horizontally in some uprights made such that the rod can be rotated. In addition to the rod holder, you will need to make something to hold and distribute the thread to the rod. You will also need a motorized device and carriage to rotate the rod slowly as it dries when the wraps are varnished. Most commercial wrappers have these motors included. Many commercial wrappers cost $300 or more. Alternate sources of parts to build your wrapper would be eBay. You can also engineer used BBQ motors to be used as drying motors. They usually turn at 5rpm, which is a bit slow, but it works.

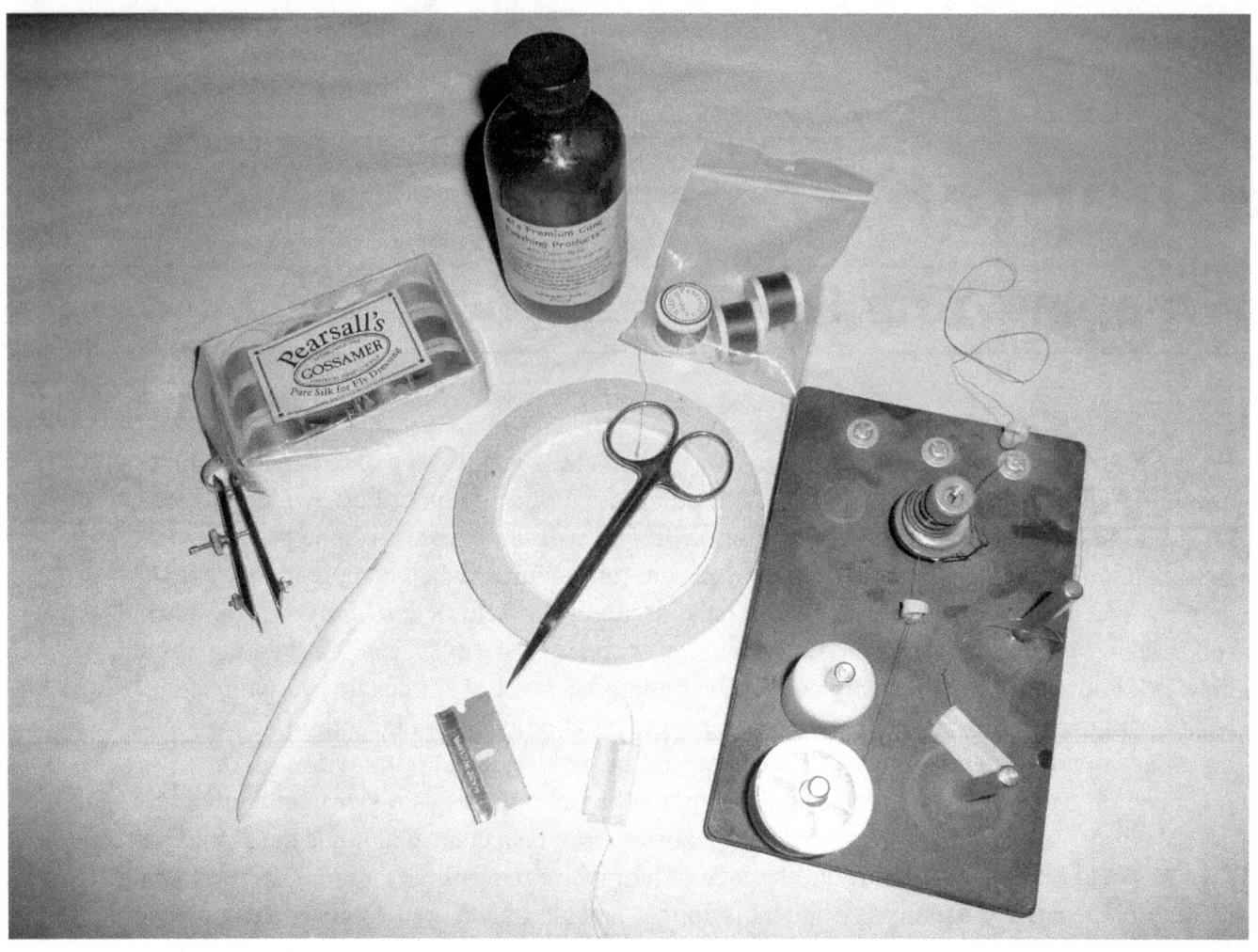

Figure 27.1: Wrapping tools and items

Additional supplies that you will need will be a burnisher, used to smooth the thread and eliminate gaps and pack the wraps together, tie off loops you make yourself, a pair of small sharp scissors, razor blades, ¼" masking tape and a small divider (the ones you find in a drafting kit).

Bamboo rods traditionally use silk thread. If you have had no experience wrapping, practice on an old rod or a small wooden dowel. You will find that a larger size thread will be easiest to work with at first. Common threads used for bamboo fly rod making, are Pearsall's Gossamer (thin) or Naples (thicker). If you have had no rod wrapping experience do not start out using the Gossamer. Many distributors sell silk thread made in Japan. One such supplier is Rushbrooke Strand. See thread dimension chart below. I prefer YLI 100 or 50, and Pearsall's Naplels (thicker) and The thinner Gossamer for trim wraps.

Keep in mind that when you apply varnish to the thread the color will change and be darker. If you must have the exact color that the thread shows when it is dry, you must use color preserver. I like Al's Color Rite sold in his line of Al's Premium Cane Finish Products. This product is available at Angler's Work Shop. I put on five to six coats of color preserver before applying the varnish. I put on more than the directions printed on the bottle to avoid bleed through. When color preserver is used, you lose some transparency. You might consider wrapping some sample wraps on a dowel or part of a blank with the same color side by side, one wrap having color preserver and another without preserver. This can be used as a color card. Before you start wrapping your rod make sure that all previous pencil marks are cleaned off the rod and the flats have no glue or rough spots on them. I do not varnish my blanks before wrapping. Begin by wrapping the butt section first. It is the easiest to do for beginners, and will get you warmed up before starting on the more difficult tip section.

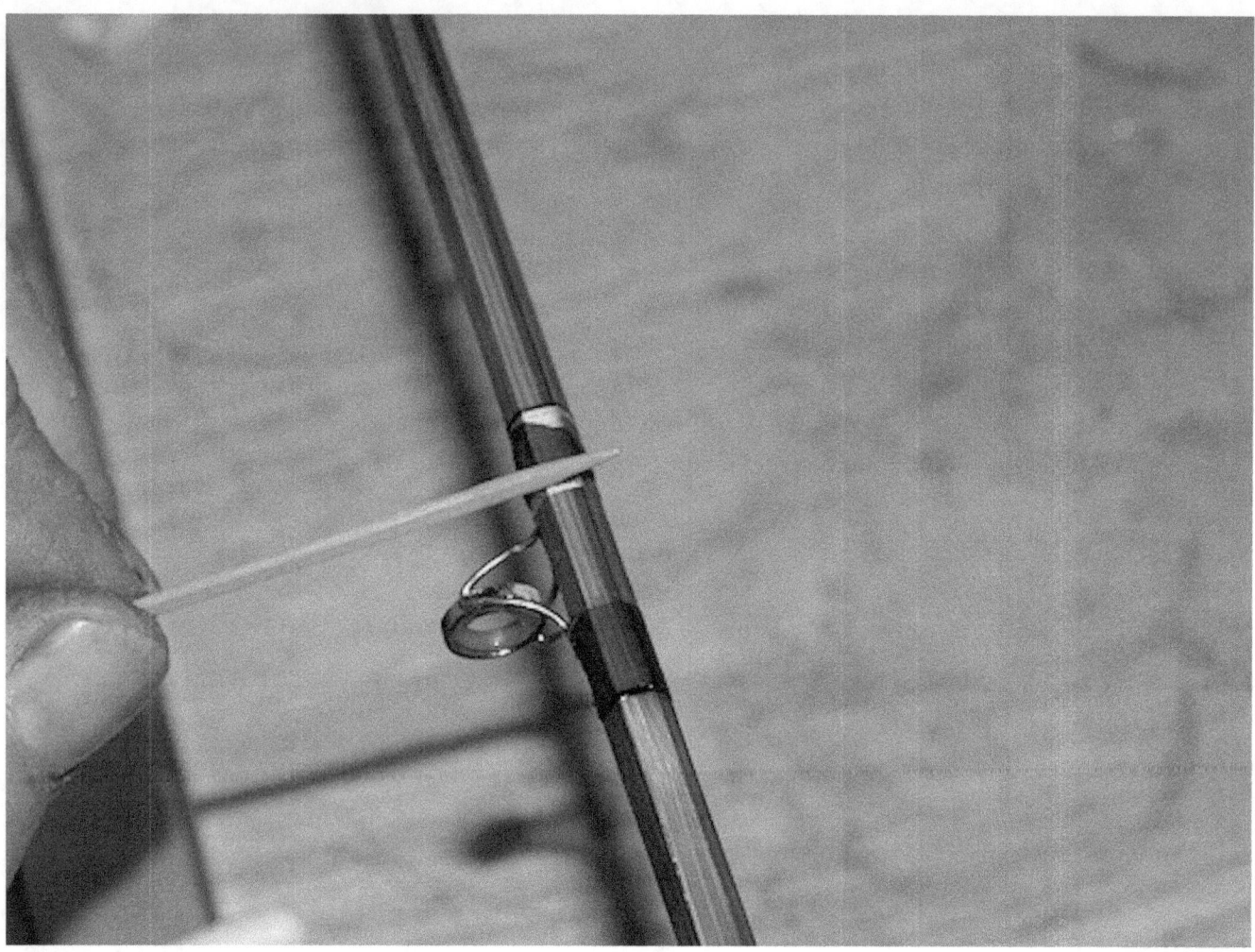

Figure 27.2: Note color change without color preserver

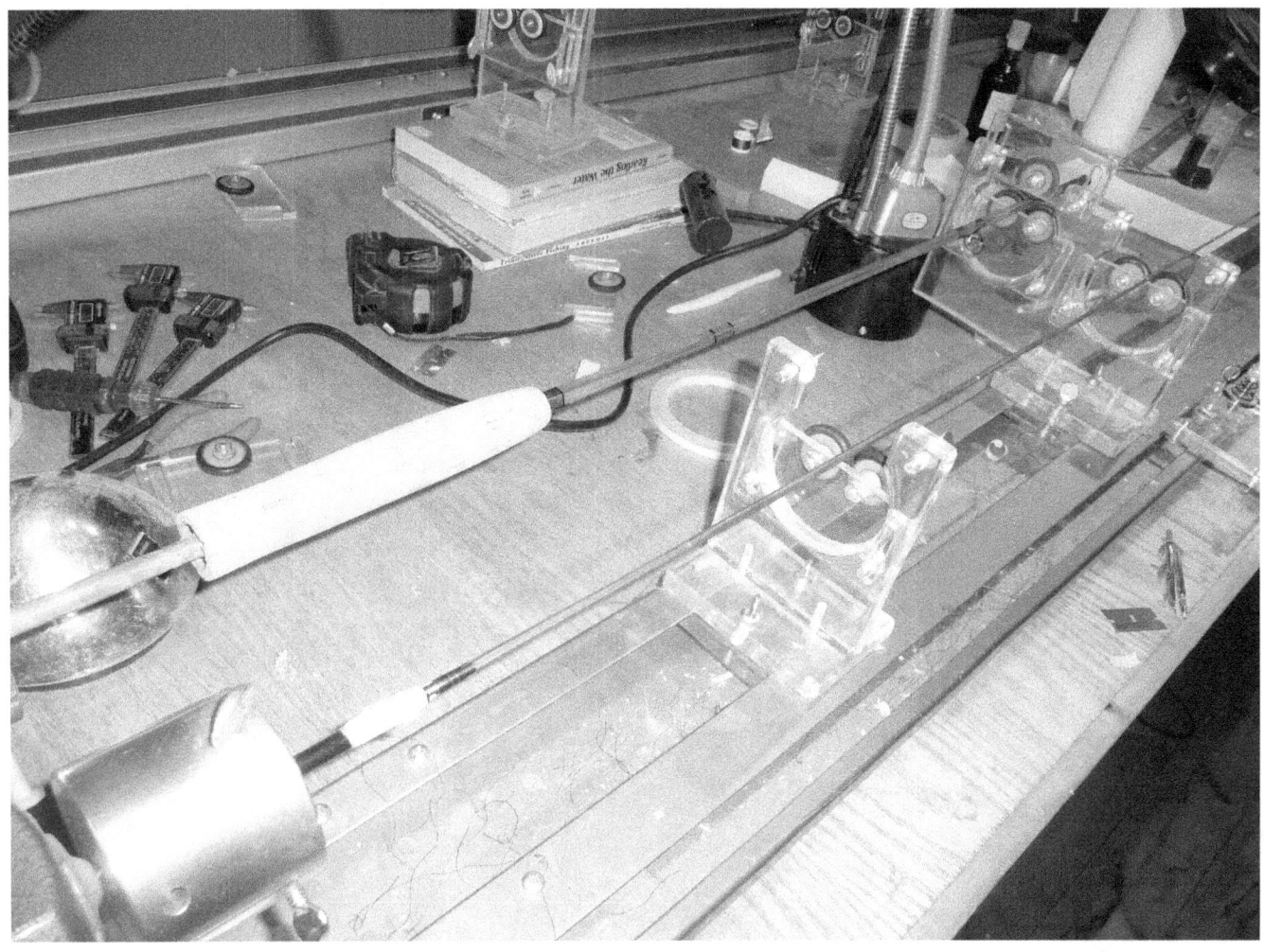

Figure 27.3: One of many power wrappers

Chapter 28

Guide preparation

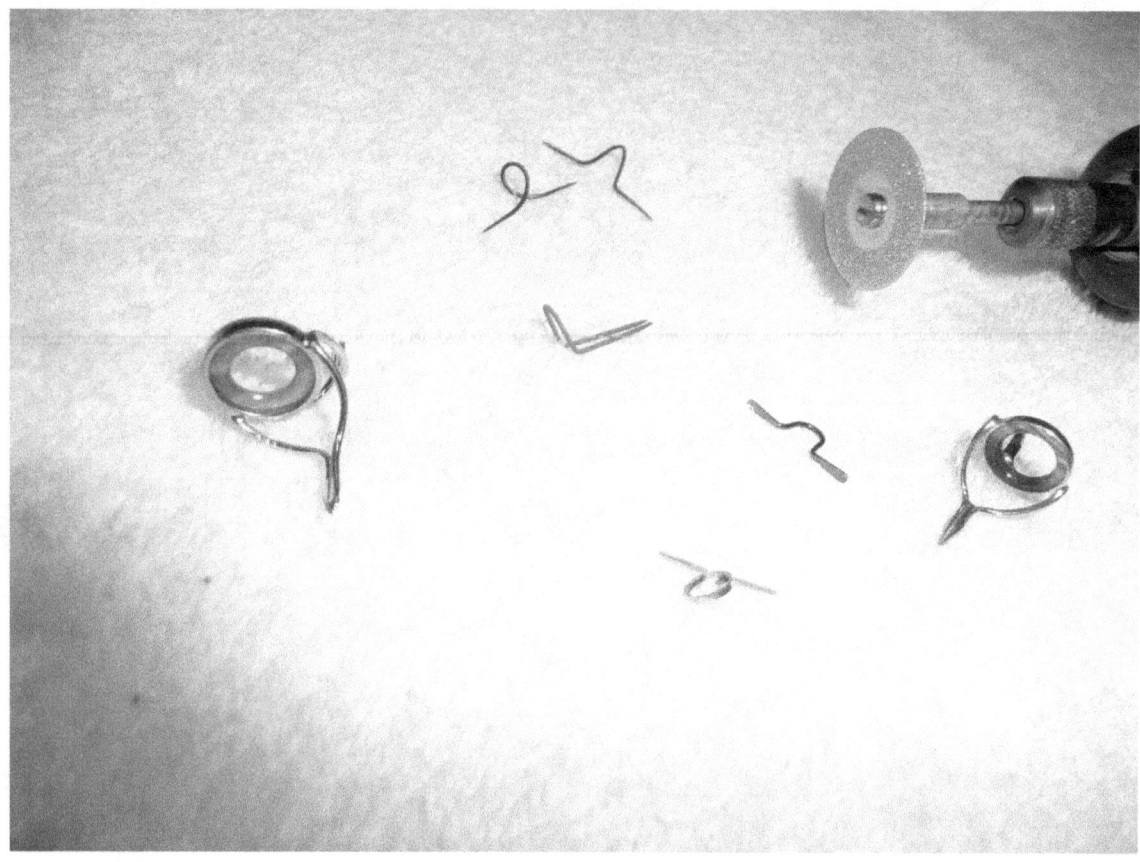

Figure 28.1: Guides and Dremel tool

Prior to mounting the guides on your rod, you will need to prepare them by using a Dremel tool with a stainless steel disc. Grind the tops of the guide feet so that they have no bump where they will transition into the bamboo blank. This enables the thread to easily climb up the guide feet. If there is a ridge at that transition point you will have trouble. (remember how you prepared the ferrule using the flat file)? If you put on a
hook keeper, do the same thing with that. If you decide to climb the thread up the cork make sure that the cork has a smooth transition to the bamboo or you will have trouble as well. You wrap the thread just up to the tip top; you don't climb up it with thread.
If your guides have been blued you can touch up the parts you ground by using a black permanent marker. When you varnish your wraps, the portion of the guide that has been touched up will be protected and will not show through the wraps as it would if not touched up.
The wraps over the guides should be the same size on either side of the guides. Wraps that are not equal on each side of the guide show poor workmanship. The drafting divider comes in handy making sure the wraps will be of equal size. Measure the width of the wrap on one side using the divider and then place the divider on the other side of the wrap. Make a small scratch on the flat with the divider needle to mark where to begin the other side of the wrap. Note: The size of the wraps should get a little smaller going down towards the tip top.
A set of wraps can be placed between the hook keeper and stripping guide in order to form a border for an information section on the rod.
Before applying color preserver or varnish to the wraps look for gaps in the wraps and pack them together or burnish if necessary. I either use a plastic burnishing tool or my thumbnail to do this. Burnishing will smooth out the silk and eliminate most small gaps between the thread.

Chapter 29

Varnishing

I use MinWax Helmsman varnish on my wraps, and the same product when dipping the rod. It provides a durable, UV resistant finish, and it is easy to work with. For my wraps, I store a small amount of varnish in a narrow necked bottle so that it doesn't form a skin over time, due to air exposure. My son likes Cholula hot sauce on his Mexican food and the empty bottle is perfect for this purpose.

29.1 Wraps

Pour a small amount of varnish from the storage bottle into a plastic mixing jigger while the rod is rotating in a drying device. Use a round toothpick to apply the varnish. (I have used 5-rpm motors, but prefer motors that rotate between 10 and 17 rpm). I do not use a brush to apply the varnish. I like to build the varnish up a little on the center of the wrap as the coats are applied. This forms sort of an oval shape to the wrap, which I like rather than a flat appearance. A toothpick allows you to do this because it can be used to easily push the varnish towards the middle of your wraps. It also can remove excess sagging varnish by using the dry portion at the other end of the toothpick. When you varnish the wraps, go slightly beyond the ends of the wraps on both sides to assure that the thread gets saturated. This technique may create some varnish build up on the bamboo next to the wraps, but it can easily be removed later using a razor blade and 400 or 600-grit wet dry.
I apply 4 coats to my wraps before dipping the rod. Two coats per day assure that varnish hardens before applying the third and fourth coats. The wrap's appearance improves as additional coats are applied. Once 4 coats of varnish dry, inspect the wraps under a magnifier and look for any tags of thread and remove them using a razor blade. I have not found it

necessary to sand the wraps between the initial four coats of varnish. I like to wait one day before sanding the wraps, which allows the varnish to harden. I sand my wraps before dipping with small squares of 400 grit wet/dry. I fold the squares in half and then in half again being careful not to sand too hard on either side of the wraps near your tipping or trim wraps. This could cause your thread to fray.

Once I have sanded the wraps smooth and have removed excess varnish with a razor, I use 0000 steel wool to further smooth out the wraps. You will now be ready to dip the rod. Make sure to remove the white registration marks you made with a China marker at the guide locations. This is done with a Q-tip dipped in denatured alcohol or Goof Off. Some portions of the marks may remain and will need to be scraped off with an Xacto knife.

29.1 Setting Up a Varnish and Drying Area

I used a spare small cloak closet in my house to dip the rods in varnish and hang to dry. What can you use?

I live in a cold climate and it was inconvenient to have my dipping area located in my shop or in the garage. My closet was available so I didn't have to build an enclosure. Fig. 29.1. You can really get elaborate when building a dip cabinet such as using heat wrapping on the tube, fancy lighting, heating systems, and synchronous motors to lift the rod out of the varnish. When I began making rods, I had a very simple arrangement. Now my set up is somewhere in between elaborate and simple, but you can get good results using a simple system.

Find an area where you want to set up your system. You may have to build a cabinet from plywood and other materials. Build a cabinet to be about 24 wide and tall enough so that you can get the rod into the tube and also have room to hang the pieces to dry on cup hooks mounted at the top of the cabinet. The cabinet should be about 24 inches deep. Fig. 29.1 and 2. If possible, design your system so the dip tube, which will be about 4 ½ feet long and will be able to go below grade of the cabinet floor. You won't want to climb up on a ladder to put the rod section into the tube. The back wall of the structure should have a large clock with a second hand and a thermometer. It is a good idea to have a front door with some Plexiglas placed in it for visibility. The Plexiglas will also aid in attracting dust particles. I put one of those radiator shaped electric oil filled heaters in my cabinet to control temperature and I installed a double tube 4 foot fluorescent fixture mounted vertically on one side wall. This will make for good lighting and will help maintain warmth.

Directly above your tube fasten a small pulley. Drill a hole on the front side of the cabinet so a nylon cord or old fishing fly line can be used to pull the rod out of the varnish tube. The cord comes through the pulley and can exit smoothly outside of the cabinet. Install a tie off hook or clamp that you can wrap the cord around, or clamp to once you have pulled the rod section from the tube.

Figure 29.1: Home made drying/varnish cabinet

My first dip tube was made from a 2-schedule 40PVC pipet. It turned out that length of my tube, which was 58 inches, just happened to hold a little less than one gallon of varnish. I placed my tube holding the varnish inside of a larger insulated tube mounted below the floor. I glued a PVC end cap on the bottom and a female adaptor at the top of the inner tube in order to screw in a threaded plug that would seal the varnish. I have found my varnish will last in its tube for at least 6 months before replacement may be necessary. Occasionally I have to thin it a bit which is accomplished by removing the tube, adding mineral spirits (remove some varnish if necessary), shaking the tube well, and then turn end to end. Do not dip a rod section for a few hours after thinning and shaking, otherwise you may get bubbles on the sections surface. Occasionally, you get some debris or hardened varnish fragments in the tube. Emptying the tube and running the contents through a cloth strainer that can be bought at a paint store correct this. Use clean, one-gallon paint cans when transferring varnish. Removing the tube and propping it up against an inside wall of the cabinet helps warm the varnish while you are heating up the cabinet. This avoids having to wrap the varnish tube with heat wrap. Slightly warmed varnish seems to give a better finish. I keep the cabinet between 80 and 100° F.

Using a red sharpie, place marks at every inch on the cord that you use to raise and lower the rod section. This will allow you to time the withdrawal rate. The rod should be withdrawn at the rate of one inch every 15 seconds. This allows the varnish to run down the rod section and back into the surface film of the varnish. You should extend that delay time by about ten seconds at the mid point of the lower wrap at each guide.

29.1 Other Methods to Finishing a Rod

I am not one for brushing varnish on a rod. If you do not want to build a dip tube and a cabinet, or should you decide to want an unvarnished rod, you can apply Tung oil or a product used to finish gunstocks known as True Oil. This finish will not be as durable, so you will have to reapply as the rod is used. It does make for a good looking and easy way to finish a rod.

Figure 29.2: Drying/Varnish cabinet

One winter I made a 7'0" one-piece rod and it was too cold to rig up a long dip tube outside. I decided to use the wipe on varnish technique in order to finish the rod. I first applied four coats of varnish to all of the silk wraps as usual. Wipe on varnish can be purchased or better yet, you can make it yourself. You take your standard varnish and thin it with mineral spirits at a 50 percent ratio. Using a clean paper towel, wipe on this mixture over the entire rod, including the wraps. Apply a lot of pressure so there is no build up. Allow about 2 hours to dry. You don't want the first coat to be tacky when you apply the second coat. Put 4 to 5 coats on the rod using this method. The next day lightly sand the rod with 600 wet/dry and then use 0000 steel wool. Again apply a few coats of the thinned varnish. Repeat this process until you get a finish that you are happy with.

29.1 Dipping

Start by straightening out a paper clip. Bend in a small 90-degree angle where the clip will be taped to the rod. Firmly tape on the paper clip at the top of the rod segment; this will prevent the clip from slipping through the spot where it is taped on. Bend the other end around an S fitting that will have been tied on to the end of your cord. Remember to fasten the paper clip securely to the S hook. Wrap it around it! It is bad news if the rod falls into the dip tank. Ask me how I know.

When dipping your butt section, be sure to plug the female ferrule. A small rubber tapered plug works well or you can use the proper sized drill bit putting tape on it to provide friction going into the female ferrule. Mask off the female ferrule with tape to keep varnish off from it. Note: Your butt section will not have the reel seat mounted at this time.

The cleaning of the section is very important to get a good finish. Oil from your hands and oil that comes from using steel wool will greatly reduce the ability of the varnish to adhere to the rod. You will get bubbles and rough spots if the rod is not cleaned properly. Before you dip the rod, clean it thoroughly with mineral spirits using a clean cloth. I like a paper towel. If you use a cloth, make sure that the cloth was not in a dryer with fabric softener added, as the oil in the fabric softener is bad news. Do not rub the butt section information area you have written on.

Depending on your climate and room temperature, you can remove the rod from the pull cord and hang it on a cup hook in the cabinet after one hour. You can take it out to examine, and admire it after about 4 to 5 hours. Let it dry for two days before sanding and executing the second dip.

29.2 Second Dipping

When the rod has dried for two days you can prepare it for the second dip. If done before this, the varnish will really load up your sand paper and the soft varnish will tend to cause irregularities in the finish when you sand it. Under good lighting, use the 400 grit squares of wet /dry to carefully sand the wraps. Also sand all of the flats because rough spots can be typically found on the flats after the first dip. Now steel wool everything with 0000 steel wool. This time before dipping, meticulously clean the rod with mineral spirits making sure there is no lint or dust on the flats. You can blow it off with compressed air if you like.

Chapter 30

Reel Seat Construction

You can purchase a prefabricated reel seat or make your own. I mostly use cap and band or band up locking seats. Fig. 30.1 and 30.2

You can also purchase nickel silver hardware for the seats (see appendix A). At one time I was going to make my own hardware, however, I decided to put that idea on the back burner when I found a friend, who could make any style of seat I wanted.

Obviously, you will need a lathe to make reel seat inserts. It is fairly easy to become familiar with a wood lathe, as I had not used a lathe since I was in junior high school.

Acquiring hardwood can be fun as there is some interesting stuff out there. No matter what wood that you decide to use, make sure that the hardwood looks good with your choices in wrap color and the color of your bamboo. Some combinations can really clash. You can get precut wood or wood in bulk sizes. If you don't have a means to cut the large pieces (table saw) you can purchase one-inch squares from various suppliers. One such supplier is Amazon Exotic Hardwoods. They have some great stuff!

The origins of your wood can be varied. I had a neighbor who was sawing up some pallets for his wood stove and he came across some spalted ash. I used that wood on a rod that I sent to PA. Fig. 30.3.

Cut the one inch squares into lengths of 4¼". Your finished reel seat will be 3½", but you will need some work around room while turning your piece. Center the piece vertically in a pen blank vise on the drill press platform. Fig. 30.3. Using an extended length ⅜" drill bit (6"), start a hole down through the piece, depending on your drill press, you may only get about half way through the piece. Stop the drill press and raise the platform until the drill bit

. Figure 30.1 Starting the wooden seat (also see Chapter 31)

just hits the point where the press would go no further. Restart the drill and continue to go through the piece. Now the piece is ready to be secured to the mandrel and can be Put on the lathe for turning

Figure 30.2: Starting the mushroom style wooden seat

Figure 30.3: Cap and band style

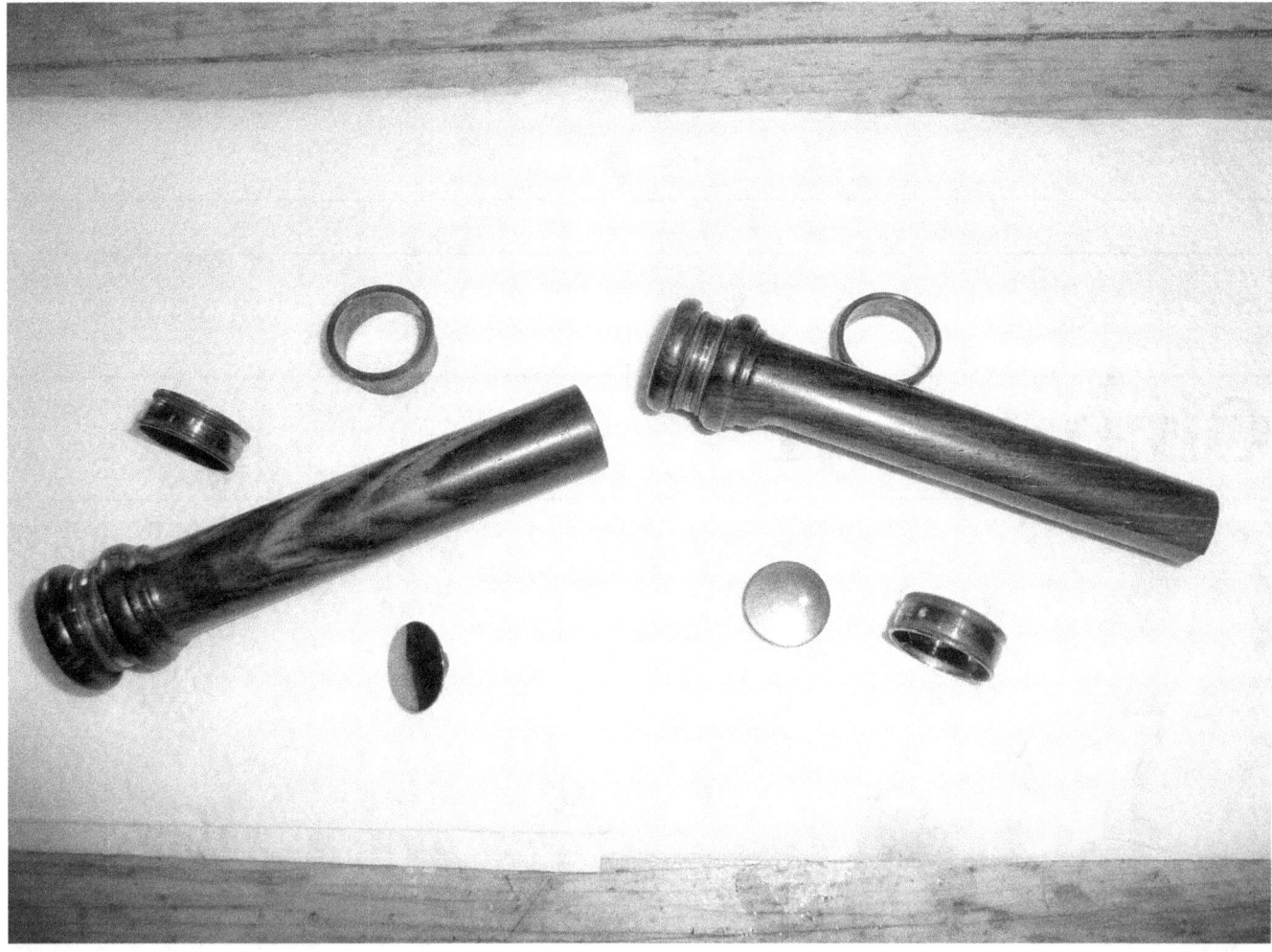

Figure 30.4: Mushroom style seat

Chapter 31

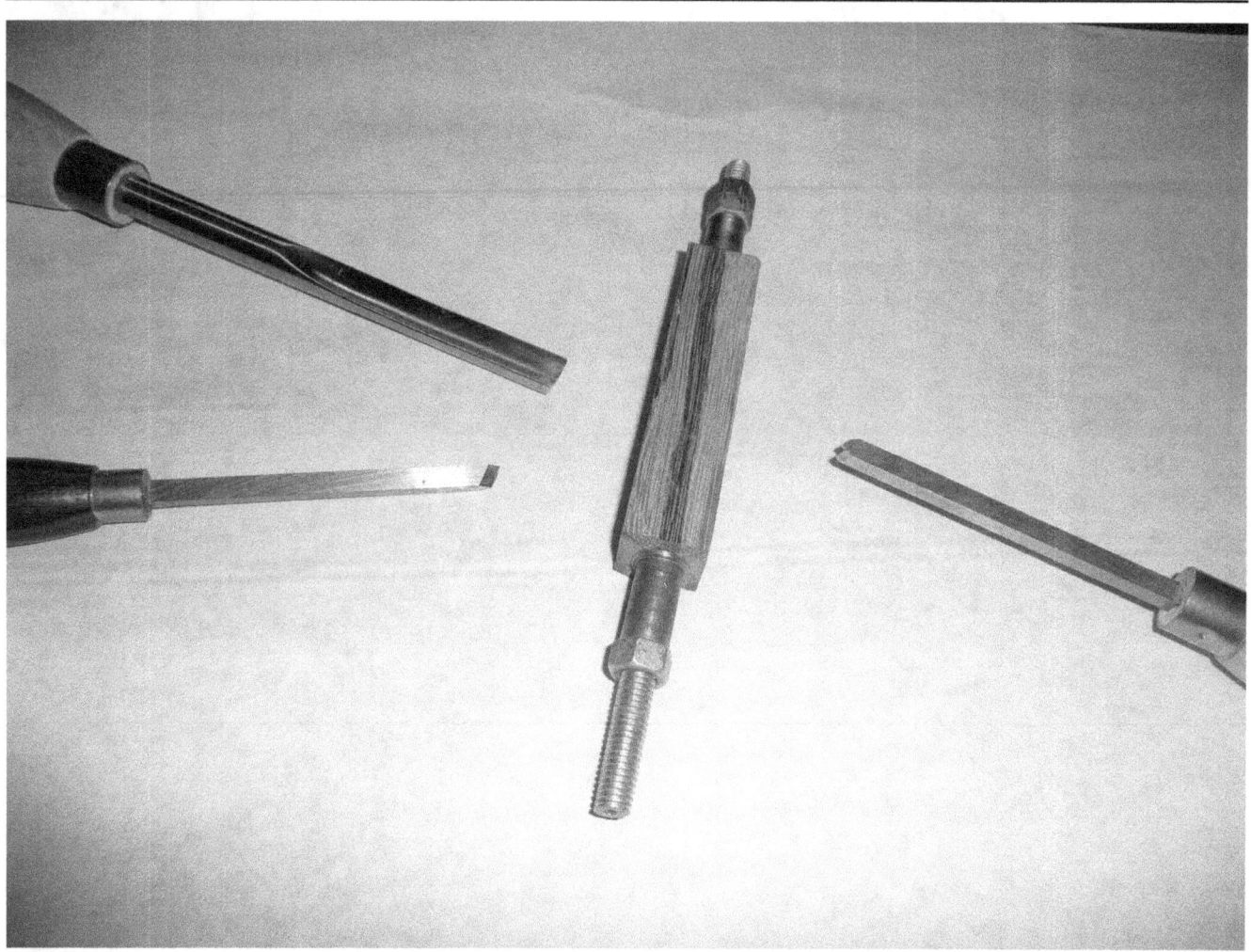

Making a Mandrel

Fig. 31.1: Mandrel and lathe tools

Figure 31.2: Pen vise for holding 1x1 stock

Figure 31.3: Jig for routing seat

152

The jig above was made by Bob Venneri and was modified by me. It was quite simple to build. Fig. 31.3. The jig slides along the fence against the bit mounted in the router, which is mounted to a router table. Fig. 31.4. I understand that he is selling the special router bits again for about 50 bucks.

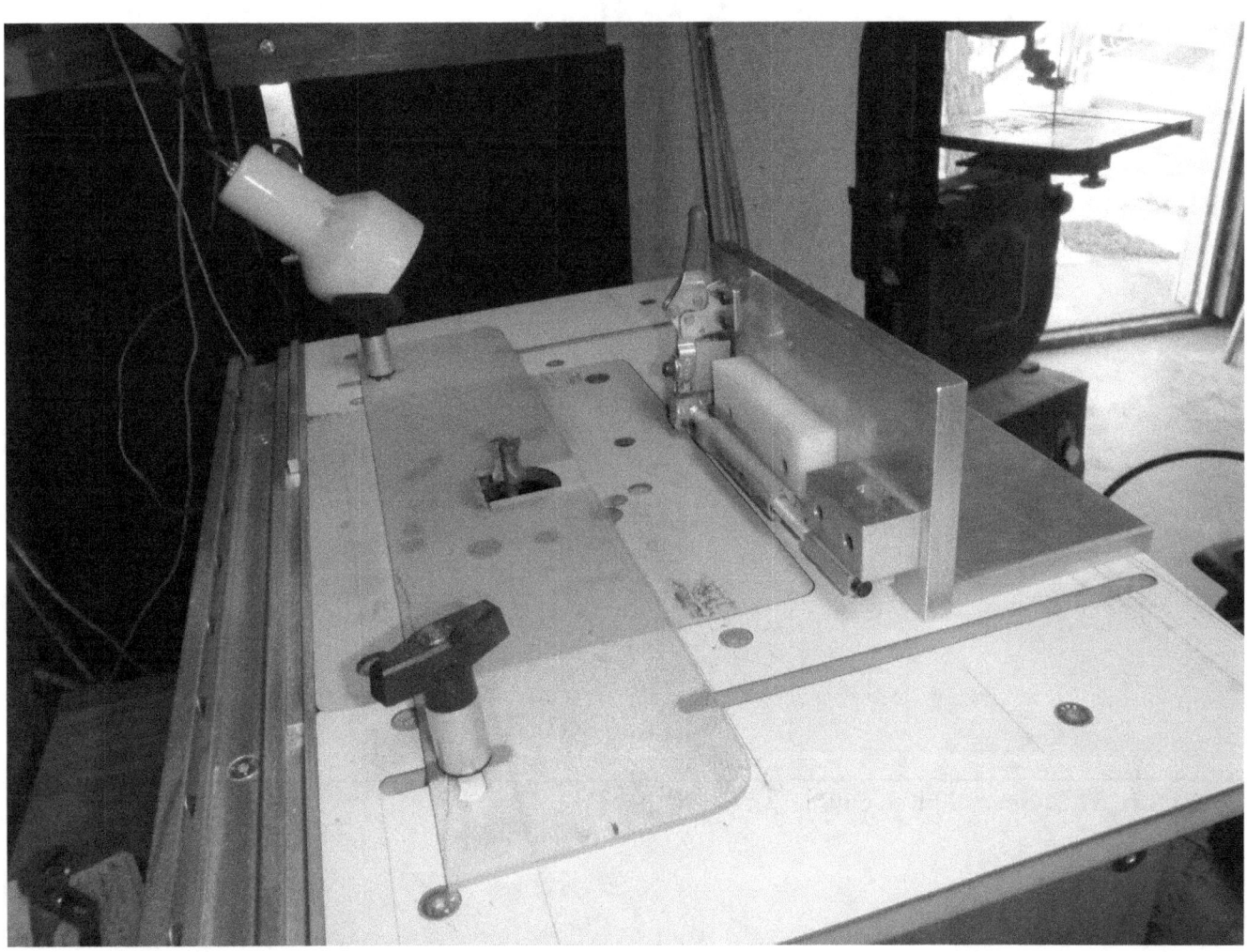

Figure 31.4: Below-Jig on router table

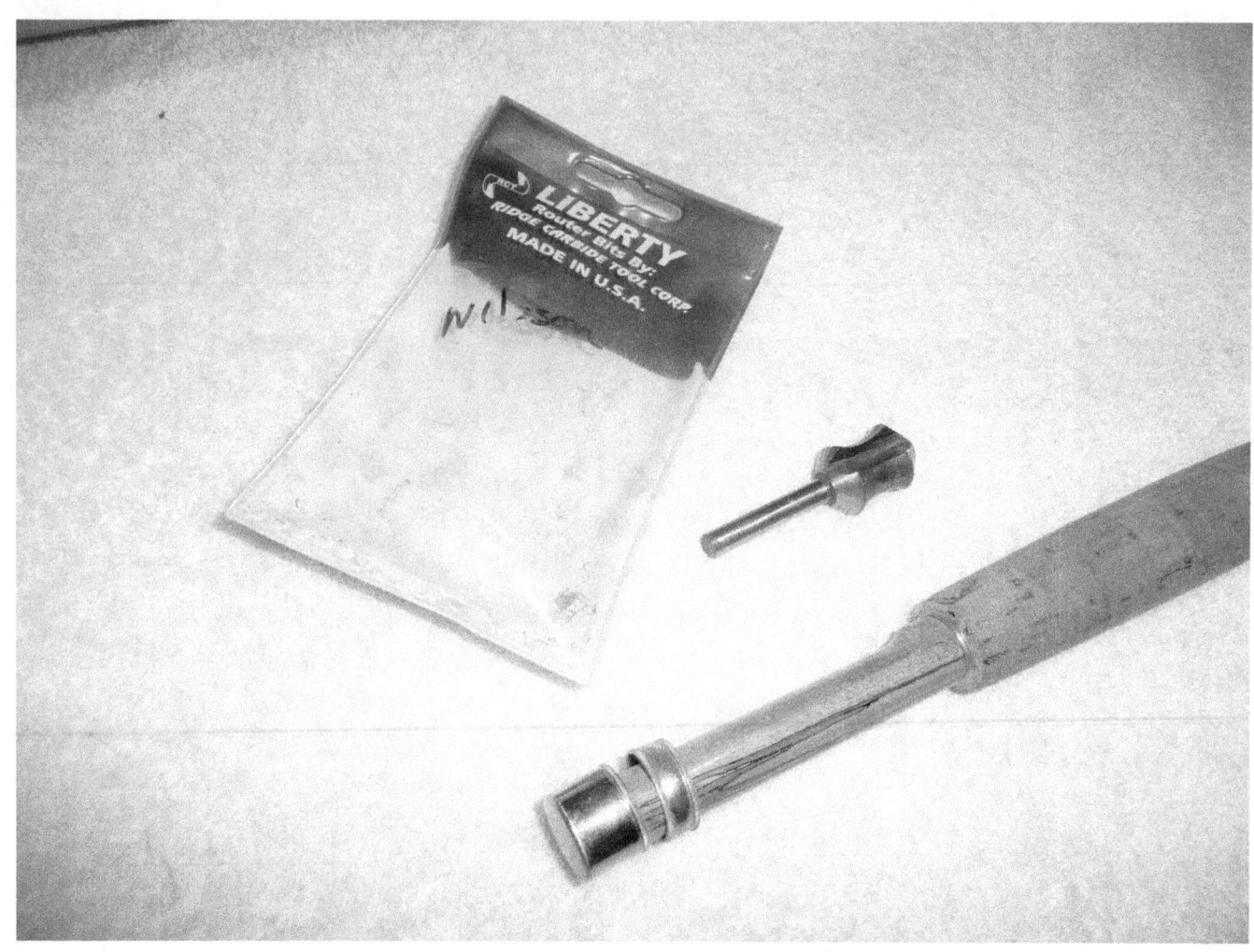

Figure 31.5: Special bit to cut reel seat

Use a 3/8" piece of threaded rod and cut it to about 9" long. Put on two 3/8" nuts next to each other on one end. This end will be held best in the lathe chuck jaws. Now slide on a 3/8" bronze bushing. Then place on your piece that you drilled the 3/8" hole through. It will slide on nicely. Put on another bronze bushing followed by one 3/8" nut. Fig. 31.1.

Place the end that has two nuts into the lathe chuck jaws and the other end of the threaded rod must have a 1/16" hole drilled into it so that the live center will fit into and against it. Tighten the 3/8" nut on the live center end with a 9/16" wrench. This will hold the piece so the piece won't change position while turning in the lathe.

While you are turning the piece with a gouge, use light pressure with the tool until the 90° edges are gone. Fig. 30.1. I use three lathe cutting tools, a 3/8" gouge, a 3/16" beading tool when I make ridges on my mushroom style seats. I use a 1/8" skew for forming the place where the small nickel piece sits between the seat and cork grip. I prefer a handle of no longer than 8" on my lathe tools.

Once the piece is reduced in diameter, periodically check that diameter with digital calipers. Your target will be the inside diameter of the cap and band.. This diameter must be a little under, but not over that dimension. You can remove the last bit of wood by using strips of sandpaper while the lathe is turning. This would be the same technique that you used while shaping the cork. Reduce the grit as you go along and end up with 600 or 1000 followed by steel wool 0000. I use a friction polish after the steel wool and then decide if I want to varnish the wood insert or just leave it oiled.

The reel seat can now be taken out of the lathe and cut it to 3 1/2". I mortise a radius on one side of the seat to accommodate the reel. You can make, or buy a jig to hold t h e reel seat insert while running it against a fence on your router table. The fingernail bit for the router must be custom made to do this operation. My source for the bit is Ridge Carbide Tool Corp (201) 438 8778. (Fig. 31.4.). They have the drawing of my bit on file under the product code 020807-1 that would apply to my customer name Scott Nilsson. That particular bit has a 1/4" shaft. They can provide a 1/2" shaft under product code 101508-1 with the name Roy Ross as the customer.

31.1 Gluing On the Seat

A properly made bamboo fly rod will have both the tip and butt sections exactly the same length. The tip should be the standard by which you can make small adjustments to the butt length to make sure this standard is achieved. Line up the two sections and make any minute adjustment at the reel seat location that is required to make the two sections the same length. I use 5-minute epoxy to glue my seats on. You can glue the nickel piece butting up against the cork and the wooden insert in one step. Align the seat with your guides on the butt section so that your reel lines up in the proper position with your striping and snake guides.

When you mix the 5 minute epoxy, have some paper towels and an open can of denatured alcohol on hand as it is much easier to clean off excess glue before it hardens. After the glue on the seat has dried, slip on the ring and tape it to the center of the seat to keep it from sliding into glue during the next step. Mix epoxy as before and apply some to the inside of the cap, and also to its sides and bottom keeping glue away from where the reel will enter the cap when it is mounted on the rod. Make sure that no excess glue has squeezed into this area. If excess glue does appear, clean it out with a toothpick wrapped around a paper towel that has been dipped in denatured alcohol.

Chapter 32
Time to Be Proud Of Your Accomplishment

You have taken on a difficult task and although your first attempt is not expected to be perfect, the rod you created will provide you with a great deal of pride and satisfaction. It is my hope that you will decide to build more rods in the future.

Chapter 33
A Word on Fly Lines

You can greatly change the performance of fly rods by using different styles, brands and weights of fly lines. Many bamboo fly rod fishers use only DT lines. I have found I prefer weight forward lines on my rods, and usually go one size up on the weight recommendation specified on the rod. Some of the lines that I like are Cortland, especially their line named "Sylk". It is especially designed for bamboo rods. Other Cortland lines perform well also. I like Rio Grand lines and the Cabala's Premier Plus, which has an attractive price. Your final selection will be based on what feels best to you, and suits your casting style and casting requirements.

Chapter 33
Care of Your Bamboo Fly Rod

Many folks regard bamboo fly rods as fragile, but bamboo is as strong as steel by weight. In most cases bamboo fly rods have a solid body construction and is not tubular, so it can take quite a beating. I often refer to the picture below as testimonial to the strength of the rods..

Figure 34.1: Not fragile

If you used the MinWax Helmsman varnish on your rod, you will have a durable finish that will protect it from UV rays, and make it quite waterproof. However, never put your rod back into a sock or tube when it is wet, let it dry thoroughly. If you should decide to display the rod, make sure not to let it sit in one position for an extended period of time (months) as this will cause sets to occur. Instead, you should rotate the rod periodically if it is displayed. When you break the rod down grab the ferrule by the metal portions of the ferrule at both sides. You can twist the sections apart if you do not grab the bamboo. As you use the rod, the male ferrule will become dirty and tend to fit too tightly into the female part of the ferrule. You should inspect the male ferrule regularly for dirt build up, and clean it using 0000 steel wool and then apply some soap from a dry Ivory bar. If the rod does become stuck, do not force the rod apart. This risks separating one of the ferrule pieces from the bamboo. If the ferrule becomes stuck, hold the rod vertically and apply some WD 40 so that it runs down into the female ferrule. Grab both sides of the ferrule and twist. You can use a piece of bicycle inner tube to provide more friction if needed. Once the rod is apart, clean the oil from the ferrule parts using mineral spirits, and then clean the metal parts using the 0000 steel wool and reapply some soap.

Over time most bamboo rods develop sets in the tip section. If you want to straighten them, gently heat the bend with your heat gun and apply pressure opposite the bend. Do this carefully as not to burn the varnish or cane. It is better to repeat this operation than to apply too much heat on the first attempt.

If you would like to clean up your cork you can apply SoftScub with bleach to the grip and then rub it with the rough side of a ScotchBrite pad. After the grime is removed rinse and use the sponge side of the pad to remove the product and dry off with a cotton towel.

It is a good idea to apply a high quality acrylic floor polish to the rod, perhaps twice a year. This will help protect the finish.

Appendix A   Suppliers

Suppliers

Agate Guides, Snake Guides and Reel Seat Hard- ware
Snake Brand Guides http://www.snakeguides.com/#&panel1-2
J.E. Arguello Rod Company http://jearguello.com/agate-stripping-guides/
Golden Witch http://www.goldenwitch.com
Reel Seat Hardware Ray Lee 515 S Hayes St Moscow, Idaho 83843 rwlee47@hotmail.com

Agate Guides, Snake Guides and Reel Seat Hard- ware
Snake Brand Guides http://www.snakeguides.com/#&panel1-2
J.E. Arguello Rod Company http://jearguello.com/agate-stripping-guides/
Golden Witch http://www.goldenwitch.com
Reel Seat Hardware Ray Lee 515 S Hayes St Moscow, Idaho 83843 rwlee47@hotmail.com

Bamboo
Bamboo Broker http://www.bamboobroker.com/
Charles Demarest http://www.tonkincane.com/tonkprice.html

Bevelers and rough forms
Bevelers' http://quinchat.webs.com/
Wooden forms http://www.wagnerrods.com/
Van's Instant Gun Blue http://www.vansgunblue.com/

Binders

Jeff Wagner http://www.wagnerrods.com/

Bluing agent

Van's Instant Gun Blue http://www.vansgunblue.com/

Cork

The best one bar none/ C and D Trading Company http://cdtradinginc.com/

Ferrules

Rush River Rods http://www.rushriverrods.com/

Classic Sporting Enterprises Sporting Enterprises As far as I know CSE has no website. You can reach them the old fashioned way however, by phone @ 802-525-3623.

J.D. Wagner Rod maker http://www.wagnerrods.com/

(CSE) Bellinger http://www.genuinebellinger.com/store/

Forms

Jeff Wagner http://www.wagnerrods.com/

Swearington http://www.planingforms.webs.com/

Glue

Nelson Paint Company http://www.nelsonpaint.com/UNI800-QT.html

Hardwood

Amazon Exotic Hardwoods http://www.amazonexotichardwoods.com/

Planes

Lie Nielsen http://www.lie-nielsen.com/

Rod Tubes and Rod Socks

Landmark Component Co. http://www.landmarkflyrodtubes.com/

Rod Socks http://www.flyrodcrafters.com/servlet/the-Rod-Bags/Categories

Rod Wrappers

Angler's Workshop http://www.anglersworkshop.com/rod-building/thread-tools-supplies/ rod-wrappers.html

Tools and Sharpening Supplies

Lie-Nielsen Toolworks http://www.lie-nielsen.com/

Highland Hardware http://www.highlandhardware.com/

Diamond stones http://www.dmtsharp.com/?gclid=CK2V18vG-7kCFctxQgodRFAADg
Center gauge http://www.wagnerrods.com/

Drying motors and miscellaneous http://www.anglersworkshop.com/rod-building.html

Fingernail bit http://ridgecarbidetool.com/custom-tools/

Lathes http://www.pennstateind.com/store/mini-lathes.html?gclid=CK670Z2vl7oCFRDZ also http://www.sherline.com/ and http://www.woodcraft.com/default.aspx?Keyword=woodcrafts&refcode=06INGOOG&gclid=CLLg1u-vl7oCFUFxQgodp0sAkA

Wooden forms http://www.wagnerrods.com/

Silk

Rushbrooke Strand http://www.roserushbrooke.com/for-fishermen/

Torches

BernzOmatic TS4000 http://www.bernzomatic.com/index.html

Silk

Rushbrooke Strand http://www.roserushbrooke.com/for-fishermen/

Jeff Wagner http://www.wagnerrods.com/

Appendix B
Binder Plans

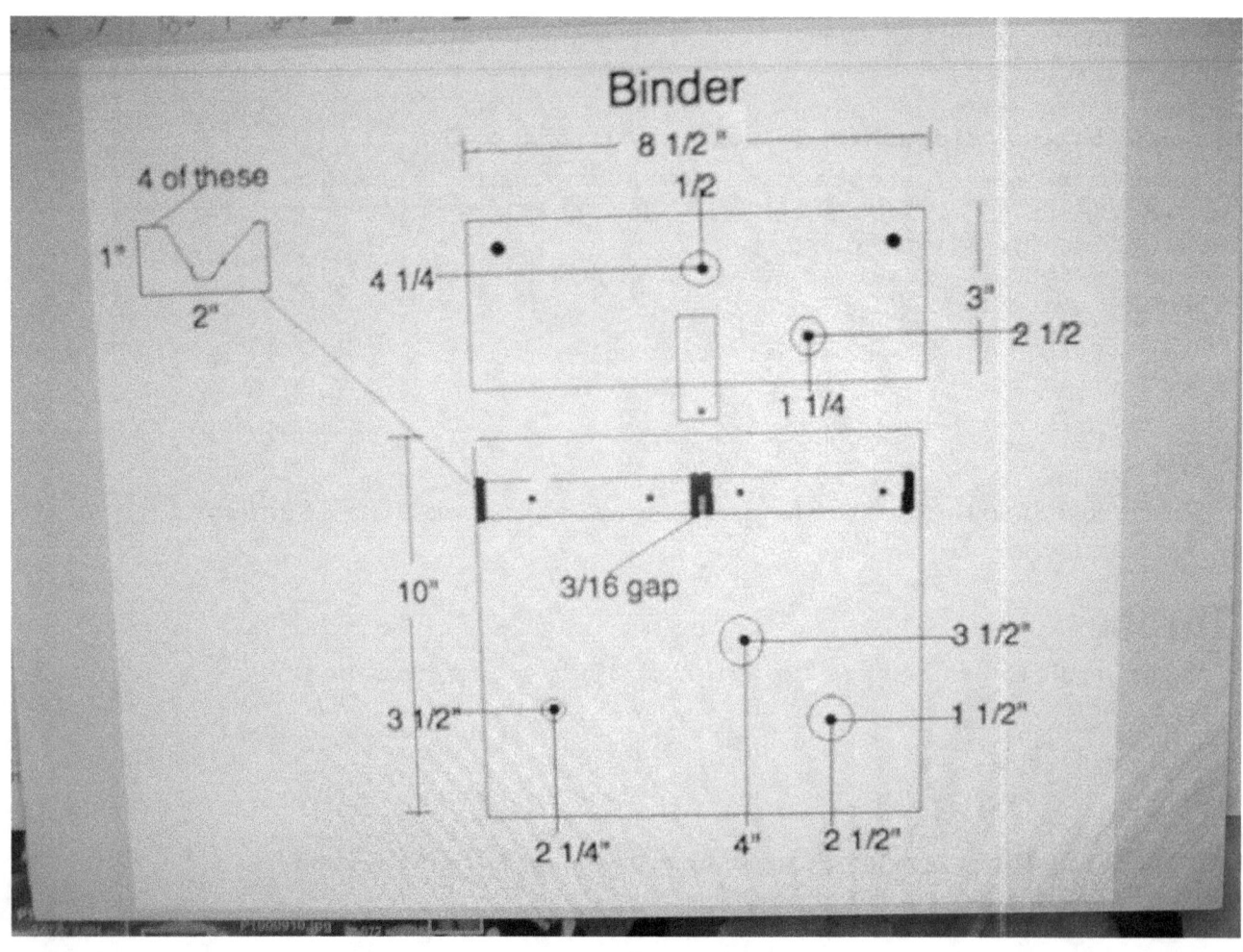

Figure B.1: Above-Tension and spool locations

Figure B.2: Binder picture

Appendix C
Electric Heater Plans

You will need these three components available from Youngblood Automation 300 36th Street S.E. Grand Rapids, MI 616 245 4111. Part number s1j54as Strip Heater, Watlow, 120v 650w. Part number 5320-175 Robert Shaw thermostats. Part number tggt-12 12 GA High Temp Wire (4 ft.). I had a local heating and air contractor make my double wall box. They also provided the insulation and glued it on. I installed the components, which was a simple task. I attached short pieces of ½ EMT to the heat strip using washes and sheet metal screws. They are held

firmly on the strip with this method and then the strip may be slid into the inner box and act as stand offs. I would recommend folding the rat wire to shape, and placing it into the box before putting in the heat strip. I bought a 4 square J box to mount the thermostat in. You will need to buy a heavy-duty appliance cord for the oven. You should buy an accurate oven shelf thermometer to check your temperature. An egg timer and a pair of tongs are also handy. If you do not want a door, you can use a large piece of oven insulation. Do not use house type insulation for this project!

Figure C.1: Heater dimensions

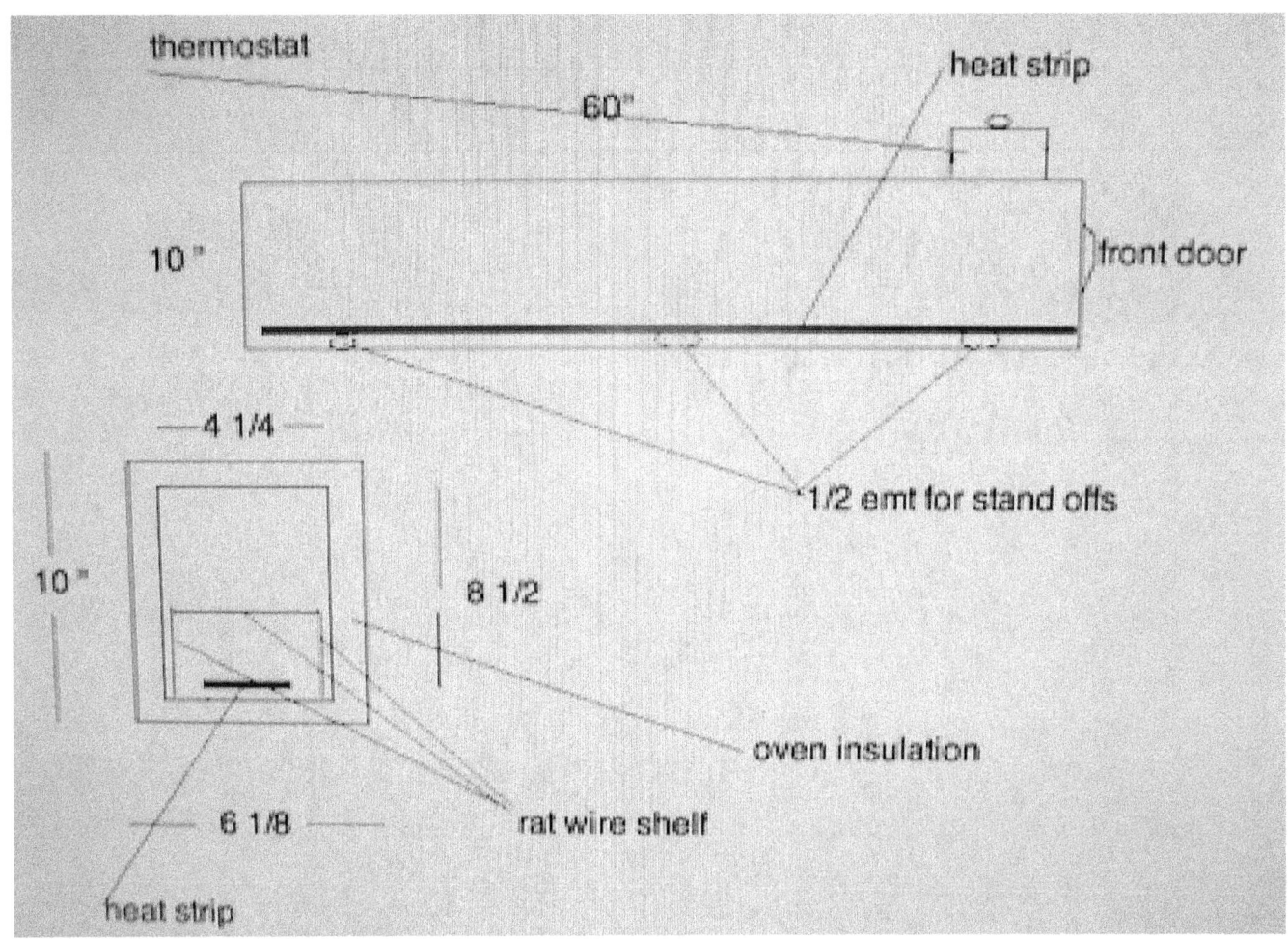

Fig. C.2. Electric oven front

Figure C.3: Electric oven-thermostat

Fig. C.4. Electric oven door

Figure C.5: Electric oven inside front

Index

Bamboo, 11

    Culm, 12,13
    - Diameter, 13
    - Diaphragm, 29
    Enamel, 27
    Flaming, 21,22,23,24
    - Imperfections, 28, Fig. 46
    -- Nodes, 13
    Pith, 27
    Power fibers, 13,14, 27,45
    - Tonkin cane, 11,12,13
    - Suppliers, 11,12
    Splitting, 25,26,27,
      - Meat cleaver, 28

    Band saw, 26,29

BernzOatic TS400,, 22,23,60

Binder, 50-56
    - X-ing pattern, 53
    - Cooking time, 52
    - Plans, 164
    Heat treating, 58,59,60,61,62
    - Relating butt to tip, 91-95
    Twist, 89,91,118

Butt, 78,93,94
    - Swelled, 64
    Jeff Wagner, 60,65
    Relating butt to tip, 91-95
    Charring, 71

Cork, 106-116
    - Cleaning, 161
      Scotch Brite, 161
      Soft Scrub, 161
    - Suppliers, 106
      - Burl, 106
      -
    - First 110
      Glue, 110
    - Shaping, 106,107,108,109,114,115,116
    - Press, 111,113,115
      - Vegetable oil, 115

Culm
    - Moisture content, 37,
    cut mark, 25

Center gauge ,44
Dial gauge,63,65,66
- Calibration,68
- Standard,63,65
Diamond stone,40
Japanese Water stone,41
Digital calipers,69,73,75
Dremel,92,138
pink eraser,70

,

Ferrules,
- Bluing,102,105
Crowning,96
Glueing,101,102
- fitting,98,99,100,101,103
Nickel silver,96
- Suppliers, See supplier appendix
 - (CSE) Bellinger,
 - Classic Sporting Enterprises,
 - J.D. Wagner Rod maker,

Flaming,21,22,23,24

torches
BernzOatic TS400,22,23
- Weed burner,22,2

Forms

metal,63,64,65,66,67,73,74

roughing,42,43,44,45,46,47,48

marks,66,67,72,75,89,90,93,131

scrapping,68,71,74,

Glue,77,78,79,80,81,82,83,84,85,86,
- 5 minute epoxy,129,156
- Gorilla,102
Urac and Unibond,79
Tite Bond,112,110
Fly Lines,158

Grit paper,
1000,124,96,97,122,123,138,144

p.173

150,89
220,92
400,96,97,122,123,138,144
60,71,77,87,99,115
600,100,115,116,122,123,138,144

Guide Feet,- Location,127,128,129,130
preparation,121-126
spline,128

Heater
electric,61,62
plans,66,167
pipe,56-61
Nodes
    Heating,34,35
    pressing,34,36
    spacing,30,31,32,33

Planes,37,38,39
  Lie Nielsen,38,39,75,76
  Stanley,37,38,

  sharpening,40,41,42,72,76

Planing
final,72,73,74,75,?
Forms,
metal,63,64
rough,42,43,44,45,46,47,48
roughing ,42,45,46,47,48
secondary,68,69,71,
table,42,68,
tips,68,71
butts,76

- Over built,87,91
- Size,68,91,94
- Stiffness, 24
- Strength,62,159
- Stress curves, 15,
- Strips,51

Taper,13,15,21
- Tip section,73
- Twist,118

Reel Seat,145-149

Mandrel,150-155

Sanding
-
blank,86,87,88
Steel wool,90,92,122,124,126,139,144,
wraps,139,143,144

Spring clamp,69

Straightening,118,119

Butt,
- Removal,string,86-90
- seat and cork location,94

- Equilateral triangle,27,43,44?
- Length,67
- Rotating,71,73
- Rough planed,
twists,50,120

Suppliers, see appendix A

Tapers,14-21,72
- David Ray,96
- Hex Rod tapers,96
- Tapers -   High Sierra Rod Company

Thread See Wrapping

Torches, *see* **flaming, torches,chapter?**
- Fine nozzle,22
- Small tip,22
- Weed burner,22,24

Varnish,
- MinMax Helmsman,139,161,
-Cabinet,139-144

wraps,138,139
- Burnish,132
Dipping,142,143,144,
- Color preserver,133,134
- Gaps,132,

Wrapping,131,133,
Color preserver,133
Al's color Rite,133
Silk,
Pearsall's Gossamer, 133
- Pearsall's Naples,133
- YLI,133
Tools,131,132,135,

-176

Bibliography

[1] Barch, RJ, *Best Of The Planing Form*,Alder Creek Enterprises,Inc,1997,pp.42-43.
[35] [2] Black, George, *Casting A Spell*, Random House, New York, 2006,pp.66. [-]

[3] CARMICHAEL, HOGY, *Creating The Garrison Fly Rod DVD*,The Angler's Club of New York,1973, 1973. [-]

[4] CATTANACH, WAYNE *Hand crafting Bamboo Fly Rods*, The Lyons Press, New York, New York, 2000. [-]

[5] DUNCAN, DAVID,JAMES, *Trout Grass DVD*,Volcano Motion Pictures, 2005. [-] [6] ENGLE, ED, *Spitting Cane*,2002 [-]

[7] GARRISON, E, *A Master's Guide to Building a Bamboo Fly Rod*, Martha's Glen Publishing Co. Katonah, New York,1977. [-]

[8] High Sierra Rod Company, http://www.highsierrarods.com/roddna.html [109] [9] RAY, DAVID,http://www.hexrod.net/Tapers/drtapers/ [-]

[10] MARDEN, LUIS, *The Angler's Bamboo*, Lyons and Burford Publishers, New York, New York, 1997. [-]

[11] GIERACH, JOHN, *Fishing Bamboo*, The Lyons Press, New York, New York, 1997. [-] [12] GOULD, RAY, *Constructing Cane Rods*, Frank Amato Publications, Portland, Oregon, 1998. [-]

[13] GOULD, RAY, *Tips And Tapers*, Frank Amato Publications, Portland, Oregon, 2004. [-] [14] PRESTON, KEN, *The Salt Water Fly Rod DVD*, Scimitar Video Productions,2004. [-]

What Others Say

I had to tell you that I took my bamboo rod to Chile for a two week fly fishing trip in Patagonia with a friend and it performed handsomely, was fun to catch and play fish with, handled the Chilean Pampa wind with ease and was able to play big browns with no problems. I love it. Thanks for your craftsmanship. It has now replaced my Sage XP as my now rod of choice.
Vern

This year Scott made me a 7foot 6-inch 5wt. It is not only beautiful but a joy to fish. I have always loved fly-fishing but now casting and playing a fish are even more special. I am proud of my Tonkin Cane rod and just wish I had done this sooner. The photos of the construction were also nice, and I have a book on my fly rod, start to finish. Thanks again Scott

Mike McRobbie
Crawford, Colorado

Hi Scott
I am not waiting any more. The rod arrived safely yesterday. The rod is a remarkable work of art, and your ability to work the cane is superb. Thanks again for the great job making my rod.
Jack ...Alameda, CA

Maybe it was the promptness that Scott Nilsson came back to me, or just his straight talk on the phone that made me want to go with High Desert Fly Rods. Well, what ever it was I believe I made the right choice to go all the way out to Boise in Idaho from Philadelphia to spend time with Scott building a superb cane rod. It was a proud moment when I finally took the finished product it in my hand and cast it out on the lawn. I believe that in building it yourself it means so much more to you and you will treasure it for years to come as you have put part of your heart and soul into it and it becomes almost a living thing, one day maybe it will become an heirloom.

                                                  Yours truly Terry F. Grills... PA

Yep, I used to throw graphite but not nowadays after Scott built me one of these

Dr. Steve McGehee... Palouse, WA

As I was going back into the house after casting for 20 minutes I was thinking to myself, "the other rods in my closet are going to be seeing more closet time that they will like because I will be fishing "Little Scottie" as I have affectionately named him already.

Chris Linck

Scott Nilsson is a true bamboo craftsman, a warm knowledgeable tutor, a lifelong mentor and always a friend. I enjoyed the bamboo fly rod learning and building experience with Scott and was never left wanting for more instruction in the many diverse skills he teaches. At the end of the class you will have the learning tools you need to continue refining the bamboo fly rod construction craft. Practicing the skills he teaches you will bring you to the master craftsmanship level Scott has attained, and maybe beyond. If you are attentive and want to learn this time honored skill, you, too, will 'become one with the boo...'.

Don Smith

180